EMERSON AND ASIA.

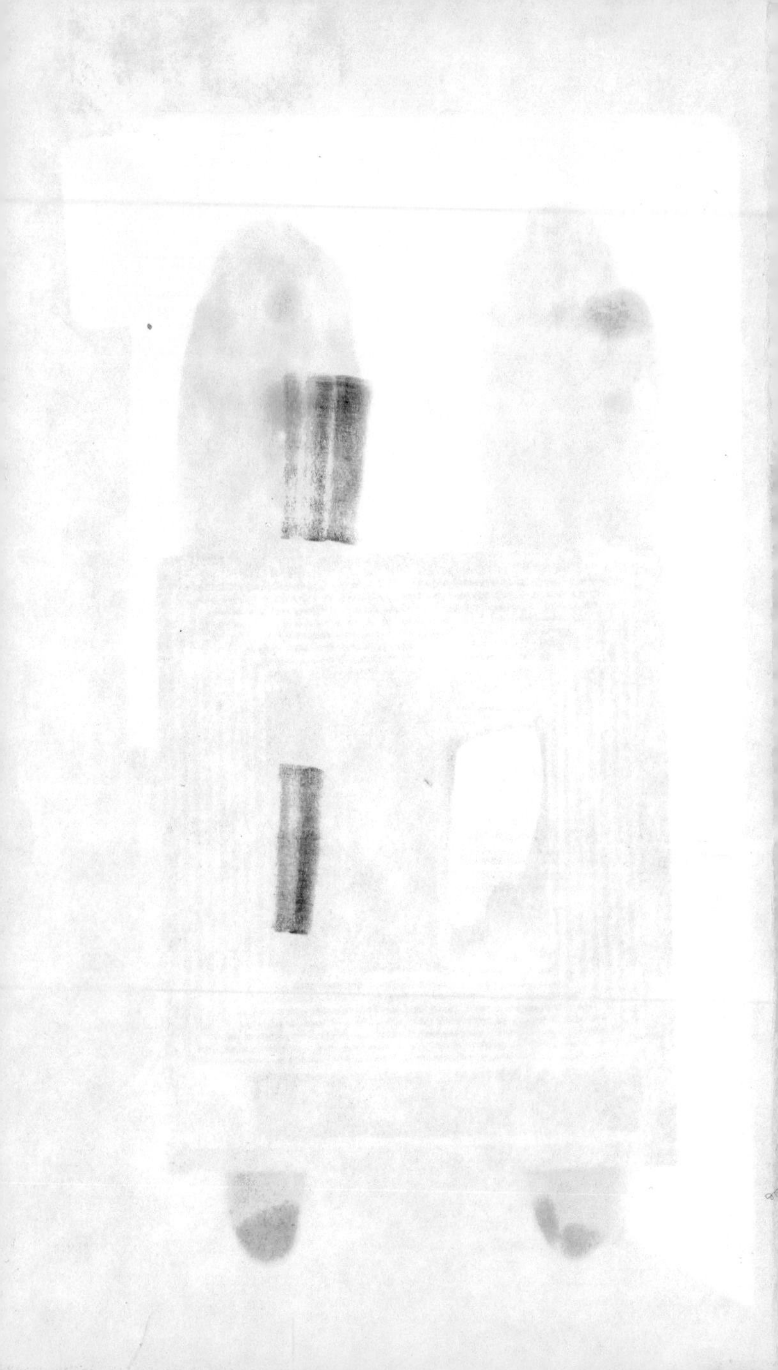

EMERSON AND ASIA

LONDON : HUMPHREY MILFORD
OXFORD UNIVERSITY PRESS

EMERSON AND ASIA

BY

FREDERIC IVES CARPENTER

CAMBRIDGE

HARVARD UNIVERSITY PRESS

1930

The Riverside Press
CAMBRIDGE · MASSACHUSETTS
PRINTED IN THE U.S.A.

TO

BLISS PERRY

PROFESSOR OF LIFE AND LITERATURE

CONTENTS

Introduction ix

I. The Undiscovered Country 1

II. "Mine Asia" 27

III. The Neoplatonists — Forerunners 39

IV. Neoplatonism 67

V. The Wisdom of the Brahmins 103

VI. Persian Poetry 161

VII. Arabian Literature and the Koran 195

VIII. The Zoroastrian Forgeries 217

IX. Confucius and China 232

X. Emerson, Asia, and Modern America 247

Appendix 257

Bibliography 265

Index 269

INTRODUCTION

TO Emerson the word "Asia" had an emotional as well as an intellectual meaning. "Asia" was more than an Eastern continent, and it was more than the literature produced by that continent. It was a symbol for the unknown — for the other half of the world — for mystery, and romance, and poetry, and love, and religion. Part of this mystery, I have tried to describe in the chapter on "Mine Asia".

But Emerson knew that the people of the Western world loved definitions and boundaries. Asia, before it could become that larger idea of which he dreamed, must be defined as the Orient. That term included for him all the lands and literatures of the continent of Asia, except those of historic Judea. For convenience (or pride) Westerners have always chosen to think of the literature of the Jews as part of their own racial heritage. The Bible has been the book of Christianity, and Christianity has been the religion of the Occident; and so, for all Westerners and for Emerson, the Bible has formed a part of Occidental literature. Although it was probably the chief factor in preparing his mind for an understanding of Oriental literatures, it will scarcely be found mentioned in the following pages. Emerson usually took it for granted, and failed to recognize its Oriental quality. He delighted in pioneering the worlds of thought, and in a sense he discovered the Neoplatonists, and after them the books of Asia; but the Bible he had always with him. "Pitch it out the window, and bounce it comes back again", he remarked. The Bible did not excite this far-traveler in the world of books, and since we are describing his travels, it must remain for us familiarly Western.

If on the other hand this discussion treats the Neoplatonists at some length, although they were not Asians by geography, the reason is the same. Emerson discovered them for himself, as they stood on the threshold of the Orient. Their mysticism was Eastern, and yet they spoke the intelligible language of Plato. They defined the larger mysteries of religion in terms that he could understand (although perhaps we cannot), and so encouraged him to his later exploration of the absolute East. For most readers, too, they have the interest of being unknown, whereas the Bible and Plato have long been familiar. Therefore, using "Asia" as a synonym for mystery and romance, the Neoplatonists were "Asians", although Plato and the authors of the Bible were not.

Neoplatonism and Oriental literatures alike deal with intangible ideas, vague concepts, and often undefined thoughts. Hence, since their materials are so vague, any discussion of them must be direct and perhaps mechanical, to be intelligible to Occidental minds. This study attempts throughout to keep close to Western reality — to date and to definition; because without these, "Asia" would again become a mere emotion. These bare facts may seem cold, and not sufficiently suggestive of the Eastern religious ideas to which they refer. Can the thought of Asia be measured by the terms of Europe? — Perhaps not. Perhaps a discussion of Oriental ideas should keep an Oriental mystery. But after all, our subject is Emerson first, and Asia only secondarily; and Emerson belongs to the "definite and result-loving West". So, if this discussion becomes mechanical, it is probably better than that it should become mystical, for Emerson himself finally preferred the "sad realism" of the West to the "melodramatic" mystery of the East.

Further, although Oriental literature has little to do with temporal concerns, Emerson himself was a modern American, born in 1803, whose mind developed strikingly during the course of the nineteenth century. His interest in Asia increased gradually during that century, and the story of this interest is invaluable to an understanding of Emerson's relations with Asia. All the later chapters of this book begin with short chronological discussions of Emerson's reading in the different Oriental literatures. These are not of great intrinsic interest, but seem necessary to the development of the thought. If the reader desires only final results, without the reasons for them, he should skip the first pages of these chapters.

Lastly — Oriental proper names always present a problem. They never seem to spell themselves the same way twice. Emerson sometimes used three or four different forms for the same name, and usually no one of these forms is that current among the scholars of to-day. The *Bhagavat Gîta*, for instance, was first the *Bhagavat Geeta*, was shortened to *The Bhagvat*, became the *Bhagavat Geta*, and later the *Bhagavad Gita*. Some writers have tried to preserve "Emerson's spelling" throughout their text, but Emerson's spelling varied almost unpredictably. I have tried to use the modern spelling in the text, and to preserve Emerson's particular spellings in the separate quotations from him. The results have sometimes been incongruous, but I know of no better way. Perhaps they may contribute to the feeling of mystery that has always surrounded Oriental names and ideas.

I take this opportunity of thanking the editors of *American Literature* for permission to reprint parts of Chapters V and X, which have appeared in that magazine; and of thanking Houghton Mifflin Company for permission to quote freely from Emerson's *Complete Works* and *Journals*.

Many friends have contributed by criticism and suggestion to the preparation of this volume, but I would thank especially Professors Bliss Perry, John Livingston Lowes, and Kenneth Ballard Murdock of Harvard; and Professors Percy Holmes Boynton and Albert Eustace Haydon of Chicago, for aid and comfort of every kind.

CHAPTER I

THE UNDISCOVERED COUNTRY

TO young Ralph Waldo Emerson the Orient was for thirty years a mysterious and unknown land. As a boy he had always hoped to explore it. Probably he never could in actuality, but he might on the wings of books; and books could give him all the advantages of travel without its discomfort and waste of time. There was nothing to compare with foreign books to widen the horizon. But Asia stood on the other side of the world, and in Emerson's day few even were the book-travelers who had ventured so far.

Moreover those who knew of the Orient had given conflicting reports. Many told of fabulous works of wisdom there. All the experience of untold generations had been condensed into a few great books. Asia was the birthplace of humanity, and the Orientals had had time to think through the riddle of the universe. The philosophy of the Brahmins was quintessential, and once learned, the scholar need seek no further. But on the other hand, some who had actually traveled up and down the lands of Asia, and who had seen how this other half of the world lived, declared that it was a land of squalor, of misery, and barbarism. Oriental life was degenerate. Its literature was a mingled web of superstition and ignorance; and for any rational young scholar to read it was a waste of time.

Emerson early heard these conflicting reports, and reacted to them sensitively, vacillating between their two extremes. Of course in his later life he was to explore this mysterious literature for himself, and to appropriate much of its rich wisdom; but he was not an Orientalist from the outset, and throughout his early life, Oriental literature was known to him only indirectly. His philosophy was formed in ignorance of it, and not until his mature years did it strongly affect his thought.

The remarkable literary fact in Emerson's case is that he was ready to profit from the reading of Oriental literature, once he was offered the opportunity. In some way the ideas that he had been assimilating during the first thirty years of his life had prepared him for it. Probably Neoplatonism was the chief element related to his early Orientalism, and that strange philosophy will be discussed in later chapters. But even that was a comparatively late development, and earlier, when he was still in college, Plato and the English Platonists had attracted him, and had prepared his mind for the larger and more mystical ideas of the Orient.

In college also Emerson first learned something of an ancient Eastern civilization that had existed before the civilization of Europe. The very first entry of his published Journals (for January, 1820), refers to this, albeit without enthusiasm: "The ostentatious ritual of India which worshipped God while outraging nature, though softened as it proceeded West, was still too harsh a discipline for the Athenian manners to undergo." — So Emerson's journey to the ancient East may be said to have begun with his earliest writing.

Some months later his thoughts were again directed to the East, this time by a lecture of Edward Everett's. The reference to Asia impressed him more deeply, and he noted:

> As we go back, before the light of tradition comes in, the veil drops. 'All tends to the mysterious East.'... From the time of the first dispersion of the human family to the time of Grecian rise, everything in the history of man is obscure, and we think ourselves sufficiently fortunate 'if we can write in broad lines the fate of a dynasty.' [1]

[1] *Journals*, I, 21.

After this, he became more alert for suggestions from the "mysterious East", soon associating "the Indian doctrine of eye-fascination" [1] with his strange attraction for Martin Gay. Later in his college career he was inspired to compose a poem of some length, entitled "Asia", [2] which he read to a group of literary friends — probably of the "Pythologian Society". But all these remarks of Emerson's contain no hint of a direct knowledge of Oriental literature, and it was appropriate that his aunt Mary Moody Emerson should have interested him in this.

Aunt Mary's advice was always a great factor in his intellectual development. She was a strangely erudite person, and correspondence with her stimulated his young mind. She it was who had said that the Emerson children were "born to be educated", and she took her full part in that education. She was on familiar terms with Plato and Plotinus, and she had recently come upon the books of the East. Emerson felt her extraordinary personality, and occasionally addressed her by the mysterious title of "Tnamurya" — an anagram of his own for

[1] *Journals*, I, 69.

[2] This poem has never been published, and is not now accessible. When the Emerson manuscripts are finally copied and opened to the public, I hope that it may appear.

"Aunt Mary". On June 10, 1822, a year after his graduation from college, in the course of a long correspondence with her he wrote casually:

> I am curious to read your Hindoo mythologies. One is apt to lament over indolence and ignorance, when he reads some of these sanguine students of the Eastern antiquities, who seem to think that all the books of knowledge and all the wisdom of Europe twice-told lie hid in the treasures of the Bramins and the volumes of Zoroaster. When I lie dreaming on the possible contents of pages as dark to me as the characters on the seal of Solomon, I console myself with calling it learning's El Dorado. Every man has a fairy-land just beyond the compass of his horizon... and it is very natural that literature at large should look for some fanciful stores of mind which surpassed example and possibility.[1]

At this same time Emerson first copied into his Journals some lines of Sir William Jones' translation: "Narayena". They appear strikingly at the end of a long soliloquy on "God", and are introduced as follows: "I know of nothing more fit to conclude the remarks which have been made in the last pages than certain fine pagan strains."[2] The coincidence of these lines with his letter to his Aunt Mary is significant, and it seems probable that his aunt had

[1] J. E. Cabot, *A Memoir of Ralph Waldo Emerson* (Boston, 1887), I, 80–81.

[2] *Journals*, I, 157.

either sent him these first Oriental verses, or had directed him to them. That her early efforts were not in vain is shown by the fact that one of these verses: "God only I perceive, God only I adore", appeared again in his Journal for 1856, thirty-four years after his first reading of it.

In 1823, however, Emerson's next reference to Asia had an entirely different tone: "That fables should abound, seems not to indicate any especial activity of mind, for, though Greece had many, stupid Indostan has more. It may be that theirs are the traditionary ingenuity of that supposed ancient parent people of Asia..."[1] This tone is explained by a later notation, which shows that Emerson had been reading an article on "Hindu Mythology" in the *Edinburgh Review*. A sample of that article follows:

> The reader may now have some general conception of two of the distinguishing characteristics of Hindu Religion, its quantity and its absurdity, in which there is nothing to match it that is, or ever was, upon the surface of the globe. We shall mention but two more of its prominent qualities; and these are, its cruelty and its sensuality.[2]

Even in those days the "Mother India" phase of the Orient was emphasized! And Emerson

[1] *Journals*, I, 303–4.

[2] *Edinburgh Review* (1818), XXIX, 388.

drew upon the Edinburgh article, noting in his Journals: "The Indian Pantheon is of prodigious size; 330 million Gods have in it each their heaven, or rather each their parlour, in this immense 'goddery'."

It was with all these passages in mind that he again wrote to his Aunt Mary, in a different strain from his first letter:

> We can set Newton over against Juggernaut.— Nevertheless... admiration paid by a few gazers to one sage's intellectual supremacy will hardly be counted in the eye of the Philanthropists any atonement for the squalid and desperate ignorance of untold millions who breathe the breath of misery in Asia...[1]

In spite of this, however, Emerson saw the attractive side of the Orient. Most of these criticisms of Asia are to be found in a Journal passage entitled "Romance", which leads to the following conclusion: "Nevertheless, Romance is mother of Knowledge... If the unknown was not magnified, nobody would explore. Europe would lack the regenerating impulse, and America lie waste, had it not been for El Dorado."[2] Once again the Orient and El Dorado are mentioned in the same breath, even when "Indostan" is "stupid", and its religion "absurd".

[1] *Journals*, I, 326–7. [2] *Ibid.*, I, 303.

A few months later, in February, 1824, the pendulum had swung completely back, and Emerson headed a long passage: "ASIA. ORIGIN", writing:

> Humanity finds it curious and good to go back to the scenes of Auld Lang Syne, to the old mansion house of Asia, the playground of its childhood.... It brings the mind palpable relief, to withdraw it from the noisy and overgrown world to these peaceful, primeval solitudes....

And again in the same passage he exhorted the American:

> Strong man! youth and glory are with thee. As thou wouldst prosper, forget not the hope of mankind. Trample not upon thy competitors, although unworthy. Europe is thy father, bear him on thy Atlantean shoulders. Asia, thy grandsire, — regenerate him.[1]

Shortly after this, he composed the following verses, — setting them between a long passage on "metaphysics", and an imaginary "Letter to Plato":

> Sleep on, ye drowsy tribes whose old repose
> The roaring oceans of the East enclose;
> Old Asia, nurse of man, and bower of gods...[2]

These passages composed by 1824, when Emerson was only twenty-one years old, show

[1] *Journals*, I, 342. [2] *Ibid.*, I, 380.

no great knowledge of Oriental literature. During this time the estimates that he was making of Oriental civilization have been seen to vary between fascination and aversion. Apparently, however, the feeling of aversion predominated, for during the next thirteen years he did not record any important idea concerning the Orient; and in 1837, when he had reached the age of thirty-four, he wrote in his Journal,

> I read with great content the August number of the *Asiatic Journal.* Herein is always the piquancy of the meeting of civilization and barbarism. Calcutta or Canton are twilights where Night and Day contend. A very good paper is the narrative of Lord Napier's mission to China.... There stand in close contrast the brief, wise English despatches, with the mountainous nonsense of Chinese diplomacy. The 'red permit' writ by the vermilion pencil of the emperor, the super-African ignorance with which England is disdained as out of bounds of civilization, and her king called 'reverently submissive', etc., etc.[1]

This lapse of thirteen years is a significant one. Although Emerson noted the contents of two Oriental books during this period, from the ages of twenty-one to thirty-four he was never sufficiently interested to make any interpretations of the Orient in his Journals. Whether this was due to the disparagement of the Orient which he

[1] *Journals*, IV, 318–9.

had heard, or merely to the difficulty of getting information concerning it, makes little difference. The formative years of his life were spent in comparative ignorance of Oriental thought. His "El Dorado" remained unexplored.

During the latter part of this period, however, his annual reading lists show a gradually increasing interest in Asia. Although he no longer paid much attention to it as the primeval source of civilization, he was reading scattered Oriental articles and books as he came on them with an intermittent interest which it is possible to trace in his reading lists. These (in so far as they include Oriental titles) are reproduced in the Appendix, and may be studied there. In this place a summary will show their general trend.

On October 27, 1830, Emerson noted: "I begin the *Histoire Comparée des Systèmes de Philosophie par M. De Gérando.*" This, as it turned out, was a momentous beginning, and extracts from this four-volume work fill the next fifteen pages of his Journals. Over a page of this consists of notes on Oriental systems: "First come the *Cosmogonies*. Indians, Chinese, Chaldeans," etc. And Mr. Edward Emerson recognizes the significance of this in his introductory note: "... In 1830 and 1831, Mr. Emerson was introduced by the work of De Gérando to the philosophers of the various schools of ancient Hellas, and also, through him and Anquetil-Duperron, learned something of the teachings of Confucius and Zoroaster. Thus he entered the path that, years later, led to the springs of Religion and Philosophy in the remote past of the Orient."[1] But this was a bare beginning, and the "philosophers of ancient Hellas" occupied Emerson much more at this time, and for many years to come.

Two years later, in 1832, Emerson found a learned article of Zoroastrianism, which he condensed at some length in his Journals.[2] In 1834 he listed the Chinese "Sheking", and may have come across one of the Indian works attributed to "Vyasa". In 1836 he read in the "Code of Menu", and read an account of, and extracts from, Confucius. But this constitutes the sum total of his Oriental reading at the time that his first volume *Nature* was published, when he was thirty-three years old, and when he had pretty well formulated his philosophy.

A study of Emerson's earlier published works emphasizes the sketchy nature of this Oriental reading. *Nature*, the *Addresses*, and the *Essays, First Series* (through 1841) contain very few re-

[1] *Journal*, II, 329. [2] II, 473–5.

ferences to the Orient, and those vague ones. In *Nature* he merely mentions "Vyasa" as a philosopher; yet Vyasa is actually a legendary name, signifying "compiler" in Sanskrit. In the *Divinity School Address* he lists "Egypt, Persia, India, China", as "lands of the devout and contemplative East", favorable to the religious sentiment. While his *Essays*, *First Series*, contains only two, equally vague references to the Orient, and these both in the same essay on "History".

This comparative absence of Orientalism in his published works, through 1841, taken in connection with a slow increase of interest as shown in his reading lists, and Journals, is important. Beginning in 1837 Emerson was reading a steadily increasing number of Oriental books. "Calidasa, the Code of Menu, Zoroaster, Buddha, Confucius, the Vedas, the Koran, the Vishnu Sarna", and several more general titles appear between 1837 and 1840. In 1841 he first came on his favorite Persian poets. But all this reading did not make a great impression on his thoughts as recorded in the Journals of those years. And as we have seen, it affected his published writing hardly at all.

A study of the correlation between Emerson's

reading lists, his Journals, and his published works, shows how slowly his mind worked in its creative processes. He seldom assimilated any foreign idea till he had come upon it several times. When he did find such an idea to his liking, he copied the significant outline of it into his Journals, and gradually absorbed it more completely into his mind. Finally he reinterpreted it in his Essays, and gave it new connection and meaning.

So it was with Emerson's Orientalism. Vaguely attracted at first, he later abandoned Oriental books as too outlandish, or else too inaccessible. Then gradually he began to rediscover them, and later to read all the Oriental books that he could lay his hands on. Beginning about 1837 he read more and more of such material, until in 1845 he suddenly became an Orientalist in earnest. But the Oriental books which he did read in those earlier years did not seriously affect his published writing until much later, and in 1844 the *Essays, Second Series* appeared, containing comparatively few and vague reminiscences of his Oriental exploration.

In 1845, when Emerson was forty-two, these earlier years of Oriental reading began to bear fruit. His mind had gradually become accustomed to the Eastern modes of thought, and in the year 1845 alone, his Journals contain almost as many references and quotations from the Orient as those of all his previous life. It is not that the volume of his Oriental reading had increased, so much as that his mind had begun to work more easily with these foreign ideas, and to suggest to him new applications and significances. From this time on he may be said to have gained the ability to use Oriental ideas in his own thought processes.

Of course this new material which he was reading, and these new ideas which he was entering in his Journals, were bound to appear eventually in his published writings. But in 1845 the next volume that he was contemplating was one of biographical interpretation — a book of *Representative Men.* This series of Occidental biographies seemed not to offer much room for the new Oriental material, but in spite of this Emerson incorporated it in them — especially in the first essay on Plato. In the process he converted the Greek philosopher into half an Orientalist, devoting a large part of the essay to the Oriental aspect of his thought. As a result the "Plato" essay contains the kernel of Emerson's Orientalism.

How would Emerson have justified himself in

his description of Plato? — Few philosophers or classical scholars would be willing to admit that Plato's mind was such as he had described it. — I believe that the answer to this question lies in Emerson's curious concept of Platonism, which, in turn, is explained by the history of his reading. He identified Plato with Platonism, declaring in his essay: "it is fair to credit the broadest generalizer with all the particulars deducible from his thesis." Further, he identified Platonism with Neoplatonism. He credited Plato with the doctrines that the Neoplatonists of Alexandria had deduced from his philosophy, and these doctrines bore a strongly Oriental tinge. They represent, historically, the fusion of Greek Platonism with a mysticism brought from the Orient by way of Alexandria.

Now Emerson had been reading these Neoplatonists enthusiastically just before beginning his Oriental reading. He had been saturating himself in their philosophy during the eight years when his real enthusiasm for Oriental books was beginning, and he easily associated the two in his mind. Thomas Taylor, the peculiar translator of Plato and the Neoplatonists, had also translated the "Chaldean Oracles", which he ascribed to Zoroaster, and which Emerson had been reading. Alcott and his English Mystics, Wright and Lane, had brought the two groups of books with them from England in 1843. So, since Emerson had always found Neoplatonism and Orientalism grouped together, and since he was giving his own free interpretation of Plato, writing as a man of letters rather than as a critical scholar; Plato might in his opinion have the credit for all these ideas which were deducible from, or parallel to, his own.

In this way Emerson actually came to express much of his own new Orientalism in characterizing Plato for his volume of *Representative Men*. But he was also planning to include in this new volume a discussion of "Swedenborg, the Mystic". Although he knew that Swedenborg was not an Orientalist, he still found in him the same type of mystical ideology to which he had become accustomed in the Eastern Scriptures, and so he naturally was led to make many comparisons of the modern mystic with them. In this second essay, also, he was able to use many of the newly-discovered riches of Oriental thought.

Finally the other *Representative Men* came in for their share of Oriental comparisons. Goethe especially lent himself to such treatment. In fact his writing had introduced Emerson to some of the new Oriental material — especially that of Kalidasa and of some of the Persian poets. Shakspeare, in turn, seemed to share the supreme poetic quality with the Orientals; while Montaigne furnished a striking contrast to them. So the new volume came out with a disguised but rich lading of Oriental materials.

EMERSON THE ORIENTALIST

From 1845 on Emerson continued his reading of Oriental books, year by year, and continued to comment on them in his Journals. As his knowledge of them grew, the benefits they gave him became more and more clear to him, and his various reasons for reading them may perhaps be classified at this point.

The chief of these he had already described to himself in his youth. For him the Orient had always been the unexplored country — the land where humanity had originated — the birthplace of all civilization and literature. As in his youth, so in his mature years, — and he noted with interest late in life: "It is only within this century that England and America discovered that their nursery tales were old German and Scandinavian stories; and now it appears that they came from India, and are the property of all the nations descended from the Aryan race."[1] In this case Emerson seems to have taken on his own rôle of "American Scholar", and to have been exploring back into the sources of the world's literature.

Besides the scholarly interest which Emerson felt in the antiquity of the Oriental books, he valued them as means to his own cultural development. From them he could learn the best that had been thought in the world. With this benefit in mind he wrote at the close of his late essay "Books":

> There is no room left,—and yet I might as well not have begun as to leave out a class of books which are the best: I mean the Bibles of the world, or the sacred books of each nation, which express for each the supreme result of their experience. After the Hebrew and Greek Scriptures, which constitute the sacred books of Christendom, these are, the Desatir of the Persians, and the Zoroastrian Oracles; the Vedas and Laws of Menu; the Upanishads, the Vishnu Purana, the Bhagvat Geeta, of the Hindoos; the books of the Buddhists; the Chinese Classic, of four books, containing the wisdom of Confucius and Mencius....
>
> ...These are Scriptures which the missionary might well carry over prairie, desert and ocean, to Siberia, Japan, Timbuctoo. Yet he will find that the spirit which is in them journeys faster than he, and greets

[1] *Works*, VIII, 187.

him on his arrival, — was there already long before him.... Is there any geography in these things? We call them Asiatic...[1]

This universal interest of Oriental books, as expressing "the supreme result of experience", was important to him.

Beside scholarly and cultural values, Emerson found in Oriental books much material favorable to his own system of ideas. Their philosophy furnished him with many suggestions which he used freely. The thought of the Hindus appealed to him particularly, and it is their sentences that he wove most deeply into his own fabric of thought. We shall see later that they furnished him many of the ideas which he had used in his earlier essay on Plato. But more specifically he developed from them his famous poems, "Hamatreya" and "Brahma". The latter perhaps marks the culmination of his ability as interpreter of Oriental thought.

The story of the genesis of "Brahma" is typical of his use of Oriental material in general.[2] In 1845, the year of his most enthusiastic Oriental reading, he came on two passages dealing with the central idea of "Brahma", and versified one

[1] *Works*, VII, 218–20.

[2] This is traced out in much greater detail in Chapter V.

of them in his Journals. In 1850 he incorporated a prose version of this idea in his essay on Plato. In 1856 he composed the final poem in his Journals, after having read other Hindu works. And in November, 1857, he published it in the *Atlantic Monthly*. — By this last date, however, Emerson had so completely absorbed the Oriental books that he had been reading that their philosophy had become blended with his own. It is this pertinence of their thought to his, that furnished Emerson's third reason for reading them.

Finally, parallel with this philosophic interest, may be listed the poetic stimulation and enjoyment which Emerson derived from the Persian poets in particular, and from the poetic quality of all Oriental literature in general. In most ways this interest was less important than that of Oriental philosophy, but perhaps it has been more generally recognized, because Emerson acknowledged it more specifically, and wrote more articles and poems as a result of it. He did not, however, make the discovery of the Persian poets till after he had to some extent sampled every other type of Oriental literature. He came upon them in 1841 in a German translation, and in the next year wrote his poem "Saadi" for

The Dial. He continued to read and translate from them at intervals; two rough translations appearing in his first volume of poems, in 1847. In 1858 he published his well-known essay on "Persian Poetry" in the *Atlantic*; and finally in 1865 he wrote a "Preface" for the first American edition of Saadi's *Gulistan*. In this latter he ascribed to Saadi the quality which, perhaps, he most valued in all Oriental poetry, saying: "(Saadi) has that splendor of expression which alone, without wealth of thought, sometimes constitutes a poet, and forces us to ponder the problem of style."[1] It is this "splendor of expression", and the mental stimulation resulting from it, that attracted Emerson so strongly to Persian poetry, and to Oriental literature in general.

These various qualities all served to lead him to a more and more complete knowledge of Oriental literature. In the 1850's this knowledge had become securely established in his mind, and began to appear strikingly in his writings. About this time, also, he began to keep a separate Journal called "The Orientalist", where he entered all quotations and ideas relating to the Orient.

[1] *The Gulistan or Rose Garden of Saadi*, translated by Francis Gladwin (Boston: Ticknor and Fields, 1865), p. ix.

Here he brought together the philosophy of India, the poetry of Persia and Arabia, and the wisdom of all the Oriental countries at once. And from this source he drew much of the richness which he was to put into his later essays.

During these same years Emerson was helping to encourage the interest in Orientalism which was slowly spreading in New England over the mid-century. In 1842–43 he had joined with Thoreau in publishing a series of "Ethnical Scriptures" (selections from the different sacred books of the Orient) in *The Dial.* During the next ten years he wrote at times to various friends discussing new Oriental books. In 1855 and 1856 he had occasion to write at length to two particular friends who had sent him books of their own on the Orient. First he addressed Lydia Maria Child to thank her for her book, *The Progress of Religious Ideas*, which contained chapters on "Hindustan, Egypt, China, Chaldea, Persia"; mentioning "all the wealth that their 'Contents' and my dipping into the Indian portion assure me..."[1] The next year he wrote at length to William Rounsville Alger to thank him for his collection of *Poetry of the East*, saying: "The enterprise is very welcome to me, this

[1] *Journal of English and Germanic Philology*, XXVI, 482.

brave sally into Orientalism, and the attempt to popularize some of its richest jewels. And yet I own to some caprices or alternation of feeling on that subject. When it was proposed to me to reprint 'the Bhagvat' in Boston, I shrank back and asked time... It would however be as neglected a book, if the Harpers published it, as it is now in the libraries..."[1] In spite of this uncertainty, however, it should be remembered that Emerson did write the Preface to Saadi's *Gulistan* when it was published several years later.

Thus, during the general period from 1850 to 1860 Emerson was widely interested in Oriental literature in every way. The depth of this interest is only discovered by a close reading of his essays on *The Conduct of Life.*

This volume was published in 1860, when Emerson was fifty-seven, and constitutes logically the conclusion and fulfilment of his life work. It contains his most mature wisdom. It rounds out the series of essays that he had begun with *Nature* in 1836. And he introduces this last volume significantly with his essay on "Fate", and concludes it with that on "Illusions". These two deal most directly and fully with Oriental ideas, and are filled with quotations

[1] *Journal of English and Germanic Philology*, XXVI, 483.

from the Orient, woven in to illustrate the very central current of the thought. Indian fables develop the Mohammedan feeling for Fatalism, and Persian verses help to bring out the Hindu conception of Illusion. Between these terminal essays, too, are numerous Oriental quotations and ideas, especially in the discussions of "Worship" and "Beauty". This final book is shot through with the colors of Oriental thought.

But Emerson did not merely accept Oriental ideas; he transmuted them. He used them to illustrate and give substance to his own thought. His essay on "Fate" argues to the conclusion that the fatal laws of the world may also be turned to man's advantage, once they are realized and accepted. And this whole essay is capped by the succeeding essay on "Power", which develops the idea of Freedom, and urges it much more conclusively. Finally, the closing essay on "Illusions" suggests the beneficent force of the illusions of the world, by the understanding of which man may gain a new sight of "the gods sitting there on their thrones."

This ability to interpret Oriental ideas in his own way Emerson kept throughout the rest of his life, and used in the scattering essays which were gathered together at intervals into his later volumes. When Thoreau died in 1862, Emerson received a bequest of about twenty Oriental books from his friend's library, most of which he read during the remaining years of his life. His late essays on "Immortality" and on "The Superlative", especially, contain passages incorporating this new Oriental material. His later Journals show a steady interest in it, and his reading-lists contain perhaps more Oriental titles, in comparison to the volume of his reading, than before.

At the very end of his published Journals occurs a passage which seems most striking of all. It sounds a closing note over the ten volumes of selections, and although Emerson himself did not write it, his son, Mr. Edward Emerson, added it as an appropriate valedictory.

> To the readers of these Journals...the words of the East Indian Mozoomdar may seem appropriate:
>
> "Yes, Emerson had all the wisdom and spirituality of the Brahmans. Brahmanism is an acquirement, a state of being rather than a creed." — "And in that sense," Mozoomdar added, "Emerson was the best of Brahmans." [1]

But this statement is of limited applicability. Emerson was the best of Brahmins only in one

[1] *Journals*, X, 476. Quoted from an address by Mozoomdar in *On the Genius and Character of Emerson*, p. 371.

sense. Like them, he had acquired wisdom and spirituality — partly from their own books. He had reinterpreted their ideas in his essays and poems. But he had *re*-interpreted them. His wisdom and spirituality were different from theirs. "We read the Orientals, but remain Occidental",[1] he wrote in 1857. And so, although like the Brahmins Emerson had achieved "a state of being rather than a creed", and although he also had gained "wisdom and spirituality", he was, and remains, Occidental.

[1] *Journals*, IX, 116.

CHAPTER II

"MINE ASIA"

AS we have seen, Emerson had always been vaguely attracted to Asia as an El Dorado or wonderland of literature and philosophy. It was the distant country whose very strangeness was fascinating. It was the other half of the world, proverbially unknown to the dwellers of the West. It was the primeval source of civilization. As a boy it had stimulated his imagination and inspired him with large and vague ideas. But to his great credit, he never attempted to describe these early ideas, or to publish them. He never wrote except of things that he knew, and until he was over forty he never really knew the literature of the Orient. Nevertheless, as he loved to generalize, it was natural that when from the solid basis of his reading he did write about the Orient, he attempted to set forth the larger truths concerning it.

These generalizations which Emerson made concerning what he vaguely called "Asia" are among the most interesting in his writings. Asia and Europe, Orient and Occident, the East and the West, are always contrasted and usually made complementary to each other. Each occupies half the world, and it is provincial in one to ignore the other. In his volume on *English Traits* he took the English as typical of the West, and wrote:

> By the law of contraries, I look for an irresistible taste for Orientalism in Britain. For a self-conceited modish life, made up of trifles, clinging to corporeal civilization, hating ideas, there is no remedy like the Oriental largeness. That astonishes and disconcerts English decorum. For once, there is thunder it never heard, light it never saw....[1]

But the Orient was not something romantically marvelous, and Emerson usually expressed an equal dislike for the provinciality, or half-ness of the East as for that of the West. His praises of the Orient are more often quoted than his criticisms, because they are more striking; but they are seldom one-sided. In his "Plato" essay he once and for all differentiated between his concepts of Asia and of Europe. These passages express both sides of the question, and contain the kernel of his thought:

> The country of unity, of immovable institutions, the seat of a philosophy delighting in abstractions, of

[1] *Works*, V, 258.

men faithful in doctrine and in practice to the idea of a deaf, unimplorable, immense fate, is Asia; and it realizes this faith in the social institution of caste. On the other side, the genius of Europe is active and creative: it resists caste by culture; its philosophy was a discipline; it is a land of arts, inventions, trade, freedom. If the East loved infinity, the West delighted in boundaries.

... Plato, in Egypt and in Eastern pilgrimages, imbibed the idea of one Deity, in which all things are absorbed. The unity of Asia and the detail of Europe; the infinitude of the Asiatic soul and the definite, result-loving, surface-seeking, opera-going Europe, — Plato came to join, and, by contact, to enhance the energy of each. The excellence of Europe and Asia are in his brain.[1]

And again:

Plato apprehended the cardinal facts. He could prostrate himself on the earth and cover his eyes whilst he adored that which cannot be numbered, or gauged, or known, or named... No man ever more fully acknowledged the Ineffable. Having paid his homage, as for the human race, to the Illimitable, he then stood erect, and for the human race affirmed, "And yet things are knowable!" — that is, the Asia in his mind was first heartily honored, — the ocean of love and power, before form, before will, before knowledge, the Same, the Good, the One; and now, refreshed and empowered by this worship, the instinct

[1] *Works*, IV, 52–54. The fundamental distinction between Asia as the country of unity, and Europe as the country of variety, Emerson had found in Victor Cousin, *Introduction to the History of Philosophy*, p. 42 ff.

of Europe, namely culture, returns; and he cries, "Yet things are knowable!"[1]

Certain phrases recall themselves from these descriptions: "The unity of Asia...the infinitude of the Asiatic soul...the Ineffable...the Asia in his mind — the ocean of love and power..." All are vague, but all have the same connotation, both for writer and for reader, and perhaps this connotative quality is the most important of all. Emerson was always trying to realize for himself what Orientalism meant; and he knew that the emotional element in it was strong. — Perhaps a chance entry in his Journals for 1837, when he was first beginning to read Oriental books, will throw more light than many pages of quotation:

> Can you not show the man of genius that always genius is situated in the world as it is with him?
>
> Lidian Emerson.
> Waldo Emerson.
> R. Waldo Emerson.
>
> I have come no farther in my query than this, when mine Asia came in and wrote her name, her son's and her husband's to warm my cold page.[2]

One of Emerson's names for Lidian Emerson, his wife, was "Mine Asia". Was she not also mysterious and fascinating to him? Did she not also belong to the other half of the world? — East

[1] *Works*, IV, 61–62. [2] *Journals*, IV, 182.

and West, Asia and Europe, Woman and Man, the feminine and the masculine principles — were they not all names for the same two poles of Nature — the same two elements of life?

And so, later, in 1843, we find a Journal passage (sandwiched between discussions of "Ward's Chinese Book", Proclus, Swedenborg, and later "Buddhism") describing a conversation on Woman and the "true sex" of minds. "The finest people marry the two sexes in their own person... It was agreed that in every act should appear the married pair: the two elements should mix in every act." [1] And the year before he had noted: "Always there is this Woman as well as this Man in the mind; Affection as well as Intellect." [2]

These two are "the gods of the mind. By religion he (the scholar) tends to unity; by intellect ... to the many.... The unity of Asia and the detail of Europe... — Plato came to join... The excellence of Europe and Asia are in his brain." [3] The feminine and the masculine principles, the two poles of Nature, the one half and the other half of the world, — both are necessary to the wholeness of things. By understanding these

[1] *Journals*, VI, 378. [2] *Ibid.*, 192.
[3] *Works*, IV, 52–54.

two the scholar may realize an essential law of the world.

Emerson tried again and again to describe this duality under its different forms. He always contrasted Asia with Europe, but his terms changed, and his descriptions of the Oriental principle altered. In general Asia is the feminine, the passive, the religious, the contemplative, "the ocean of love and power"; while Europe is the active, the practical, the definite, the inventive. The distinctions are not always clear, and sometimes the one principle is preferred, and sometimes the other. Often the feminine analogy is forgotten. But Asia is always the land of unity and contemplation — the land where only the elemental questions of life are important.

So Emerson differentiated between two mental types, saying: "Some men have the perception of difference predominant, and are conversant with surfaces and trifles; these are the men of talent.... And other men abide by the perception of Identity; these are the Orientals, the philosophers, the men of faith and divinity, the men of genius."[1] Plato, of course, was a man of genius, for he "apprehended the cardinal facts". The simple, elemental quality of life, which can

[1] *Journals*, VI, 493–4.

be comprehended only by intuition was something peculiarly Oriental. The Oriental mind was not troubled by practical details and minutiae. It cared only for the elemental things. And so "In looking at Menu and Saadi and Bhagavat, life seems in the East a simpler affair,—only a tent, and a little rice, and ass's milk; and not, as with us, what commerce has made it, a feast whose dishes come from the equator and both poles." [1]

This simplification of life makes possible a larger sweep of thought, a more clear perception. In his essay on "Persian Poetry" Emerson wrote: "The favor of the climate, making subsistence easy and encouraging an out-door life, allows to the Eastern nations a highly intellectual organization..." But this brings with it its own disadvantages, and "Life in the East wants the complexity of European and American existence; and in their writing a certain monotony betrays the poverty of the landscape, and of the social conditions. We fancy we are soon familiar with all their images." [2] Yet this monotony is only the other aspect of the Eastern Unity. This very simplicity is what makes possible a "highly intellectual organization". "Life in the East is

[1] *Journals*, VII, 242.

[2] "Preface" to the *Gulistan*, p. v.

fierce, short, hazardous, and in extremes. Its elements are few and simple... All or nothing is the genius of Oriental life."[1]

This tendency to extremes constitutes at once the virtue and the fault of the Orient, and imparts its individual quality.

> Thus the diamond and the pearl, which are only accidental and secondary in their use and value to us, are proper to the Oriental world. The diver dives a beggar, and rises with the price of kingdoms in his hand... The Orientals excel in costly arts, in the cutting of precious stones, in working in gold, in weaving on hand-looms costly stuffs from silk and wool, in spices, in dyes and drugs...elephants and camels, — things which are the poetry and superlative of commerce.[2]

The above description occurs in Emerson's essay on "The Superlative", where he justifies Oriental forms of thought and poetry as being fitted to the genius of Oriental life. Here he is sympathetic with the Orient. He distinguishes it with its preference for the superlative, from Europe, with its preference for the positive degree:

> Whilst in Western nations the superlative in conversation is tedious and weak, and in character is a capital defect, Nature delights in showing us that in the East it is animated, it is pertinent, pleasing, poetic. Whilst she appoints us to keep within the

[1] *Works*, VIII, 238. [2] *Ibid.*, X, 177.

sharp boundaries of form as the condition of our strength, she creates in the East the uncontrollable yearning to escape from limitation into the vast and boundless; to use a freedom of fancy which plays with all the works of Nature, great or minute, galaxy or grain of dust, as toys and words of the mind; inculcates the tenet of a beatitude to be found in escape from all organization and all personality, and makes ecstasy an institution.[1]

In all this lies the explanation of Emerson's love for the Orient, with its genius for poetry and speculation. Its poetry uses absolute freedom of fancy, expressing everything in extreme terms. Its very stock of images, coming directly from its life, is colorful and poetic. Its philosophy deals only with the larger aspects of Nature. In thought it uses the superlative as well as in poetry. Emerson generalized this largeness of imagination to explain the attractive quality of Oriental literature to all Occidentals.

The Northern genius finds itself singularly refreshed and stimulated by the breadth and luxuriance of Eastern imagery and modes of thinking... There is no writing which has more electric power to unbind and animate the torpid intellect than the bold Eastern muse.[2]

Contact with the Orient in all its forms and manifestations was stimulating. Emerson, more than most people, admired it. He, like Plato,

[1] *Works*, X, 176. [2] *Ibid.*, X, 179.

paid full homage to its virtues and its mysterious power. But, like Plato, he too repudiated it. He had written of Plato: "He leaves with Asia the vast and superlative; he is the arrival of accuracy and intelligence;" He concluded his own essay on "The Superlative": "If it comes back, however, to the question of final superiority, it is too plain that there is no question that the star of empire rolls West." And in his Journals for 1866, late in life, he criticized the poetry of Hafiz at length, concluding that: "The positive degree is manly, and suits me better." [1]

So the Oriental characteristic of using extremes was at times attractive and at times repulsive to Emerson. In writing of Saadi he quoted in illustration: "'A tax-gatherer', says Saadi, 'fell into a place so dangerous that, from fear, a male lion would become a female.'" [2] Emerson felt the "vivacity" of such superlatives, but also their distastefulness.

A second quality of Oriental thought, and one which he completely disliked was an absolute acceptance of Fate. He wrote of Saadi: "In common with his countrymen, Saadi gives prominence to fatalism, — a doctrine which, in Persia, in Arabia, in India, has had, in all ages, a dreadful

[1] *Journals*, X, 167. [2] "Preface" to the *Gulistan*, p. vi.

charm."[1] In his essay on "Persian Poetry" he expressed the same truth. In his essay on "Fate" he constructed almost half of his thought from Oriental materials, and concluded that Fate was an evil only when accepted passively, resignedly. In the Journals the distinction is most clear: "Orientalism is Fatalism, resignation: Occidentalism is Freedom and Will. We Occidentals are educated to wish to be first."[2]

Emerson distrusted the Orient for still another reason. In theory, its literature was excellent — it was stimulating, and suggested many new ideas. But practically, it led to a merely "intellectual organization", to a life of extremes, and to a resignation to Fate, or the accepted order. It did not foster initiative. Its philosophy was purely speculative, its poetry purely fanciful. It educated men in the theory of life, but did not teach them the practical value of it. It taught the proper manners for the caste which Fate had assigned. It did not teach effort of any kind beyond that. "The Orientals behave well", wrote Emerson, "but who cannot behave well who has nothing else to do? The poor Yankees who are doing the work are all wrinkled and vexed."[3]

[1] "Preface" to the *Gulistan*, p. ix.
[2] *Journals*, VII, 291.
[3] *Ibid.*, VI, 502.

Emerson's criticism as well as his fascination for the Orient may perhaps be explained by the feminine analogy. Asia, as it embodied the feminine principle, was passive. It was a stay-at-home country. It devoted itself to social education to the exclusion of practical training for the world's affairs. The Orientals behaved well, because they had nothing else to do. Emerson never cared much for "society". He could behave well if he wanted, but he had too much else to do. He must link his thought closely with the affairs of the men of the Western World.

CHAPTER III

THE NEOPLATONISTS — FORERUNNERS

"Thou shalt read,...Proclus, Plotinus, Jamblichus, Porphyry..."

— EMERSON'S *Journals* for 1842.

THE name, "Neoplatonists", is misleading. It implies that the philosophers of Alexandria of the third and fourth centuries were merely late Greeks, continuing the thought of Plato, and elaborating his doctrines. It suggests an exclusive intellectual descent from the greatest Greek thinker to these lesser Greek thinkers. It indicates that these philosophers were actually what they claimed to be — merely the expounders of Plato.

Of course this false emphasis was first suggested by the Neoplatonists themselves. Plotinus professed that he was merely developing Plato's doctrines; and the most important works of Porphyry and Proclus consisted of "Commentaries" on various of the dialogues of Plato. These philosophers wrote the Greek tongue, and many modern thinkers have accepted them as

later Greeks. Thomas Taylor, the strange scholar-recluse who first translated Plotinus into English, and whose translations Emerson read, declared that it was impossible to understand Plato without the aid of Neoplatonism. Under his influence Emerson also ascribed to Plato many Neoplatonic ideas, and, in his essay on Plato described the Greek philosopher as half an Orientalist. Finally, the only modern attempt to study this strain of thought as it affected Emerson,[1] has assumed the identity of Platonism with Neoplatonism, and has declared that "The Platonists", as a group, were "The Teachers of Emerson".

As far as technical philosophy and dialectic are concerned, the Neoplatonists were the continuers of Plato. But in the emphasis and inner spirit of their thought, the Neoplatonists were as much Oriental as they were Greek. By birth and training they were Oriental. They centered in Egypt, in the cosmopolitan city of Alexandria. Their founder, Ammonius Saccas — the baggage-carrier who became philosopher — lived in contact with travelers from all nations — from Palestine, Syria, Chaldaea, Persia, India; as well as from Greece and Rome. Plotinus, his pupil,

[1] John S. Harrison, *The Teachers of Emerson* (New York, 1910).

and the greatest of the school, was an Egyptian by birth and training. Proclus alone, the last of the school, returned to the Akademe to expound and develop the new thought in the ancient Greek surroundings.

In the complex of ideas that developed into Neoplatonism, there was much that was Oriental. There were many ideas that could be, and were, traced to Plato; but nevertheless were Hindu and Persian in their spirit. And there were other ideas that were purely Oriental.

Modern scholarship has declared against the probability of any direct borrowing by the Neoplatonists from Eastern books. In the ancient world manuscripts of Hindu philosophy were not carried about as much as the dialogues of Plato were. But equally, Neoplatonism, for the first generation of its existence, was an oral philosophy. Indeed, Ammonius Saccas never wrote any book, and it was only towards the close of the life of Plotinus, that the latter was persuaded to formulate his philosophy in writing. And meanwhile the intellectual world of the Near East was constantly interested in philosophical problems, and out of the new complex, a new philosophy was arising, founded, dialectically, on the written dialogues of Plato, but in spirit on the Alexandrian blend of Eastern and Western civilizations.

Some of the chief qualities of the thought of Plotinus which bear an Oriental tinge may be mentioned. First, his whole system, which is described as one of "Emanations", is surely more Hindu than Platonic. Emerson saw it described in the Philosophic Cyclopedia of De Gérando, from which he was gaining his first summary knowledge of Oriental (and some Greek) systems of thought.[1] Secondly, the idea of the All-Soul of Plotinus, central to his philosophy, corresponds closely to the "Paramâtman" of Hinduism. It has even been suggested that Emerson got his title "Over-Soul" from the Hindu, rather than from the Neoplatonists. Further, the high regard for pure intuition shown by Plotinus is Oriental; as is also his extreme justification and love of mysticism. Lastly, and more specifically, the doctrines that matter is merely the absence of spirit, and that evil is merely the absence of good, are Eastern in their origin and development.

Modern writers have increasingly recognized the strong Oriental quality of Neoplatonism. Professor G. R. S. Mead, in his introduction

[1] *Journals*, II, 345.

to the new Bohn edition of Taylor's "Select Works of Plotinus", (1914), has overemphasized it. But Emerson himself, lecturing in his later years to Harvard philosophy students, has given due weight to it, and has described both the sources of Neoplatonism, saying: "When Orientalism in Alexandria found the Platonists, a new school was produced. The sternness of the Greek school, feeling its way from argument to argument, met and combined with the beauty of Orientalism. Plotinus, Proclus, Porphyry, and Jamblichus were the apostles of the new philosophy." [1]

EMERSON'S NEOPLATONISM

However the Neoplatonic philosophy came into being, and whatever the Oriental elements which entered into it, the fact is clear that to Emerson Neoplatonism opened the door to the study of Oriental literature and philosophy. Neoplatonism, and Plato, — in so far as Emerson knew him through the Neoplatonic translations of Thomas Taylor, —introduced Emerson to Asia and to the Orient. His essay on Plato is the *locus classicus* for the expression of Orientalism in Emerson's writings. He often referred Platonic

[1] *The Atlantic Monthly*, LI, 826.

doctrines to Oriental counterparts — as when he compared Plato's doctrine of "Reminiscence" to the Hindu idea of the transmigration of souls. But the extent to which Neoplatonism served to introduce Emerson to Orientalism may best be shown by a chronological study of the growth of Emerson's interest in Neoplatonism; and by a comparison of this with the progress of his Oriental reading.

Emerson first came upon Neoplatonism in the citations which he found in Ralph Cudworth's "Intellectual System of the Universe", which he read in his college days. "Plotinus", however, is first separately mentioned in Emerson's reading list in 1830, and quotations from him are copied in the Journal for that year. This reading and citation probably occurred in De Gérando's "Histoire Comparée des Systèmes de Philosophie", which is recorded at this same time. A full description of the system of Neoplatonism occurs in that work, with many citations. But in De Gérando also, Emerson was finding summaries of the Oriental systems of thought, and his Journals for 1830–31 contain notes on these. — Thus his especial interest in Plotinus, and his more general interest in the Oriental systems of thought, began simultaneously.

In 1831, Plotinus is again mentioned in Emerson's reading list. It is a suggestive fact that, following the death of his first wife, Ellen Tucker Emerson, in February, 1831, the first literary entry in Emerson's Journal is a long, philosophical passage from Plotinus; and that this is followed by a passage from the Bible.

In 1831, Emerson also mentions reading Porphyry. And in 1834 he read Plotinus and Hermes Trismegistus. But this is the last mention of Neoplatonist reading before the publishing of *Nature*, in 1836. By that date it is known (*vide infra*) that Emerson had become very much interested in Plotinus and Neoplatonism; although as yet his Orientalism remained only a name.

In 1837 Emerson was again reading Plotinus. It is from the next year, however, that his first certain acquaintance with Thomas Taylor and his Neoplatonic translations dates. In 1838, Proclus, Synesius, and Hermes Trismegistus are listed, along with their translator. But in this same year Emerson also read several new Oriental books. "The Institutes of Menu", "Buddha", "Confucius", "Zoroaster", and Sir William Jones' "Translations of Asiatic Poetry" all appear in the Journals. And so, once again,

Emerson's larger reading of Neoplatonism, and his first direct knowledge of Oriental thought go hand in hand.

In the years 1841 to 1843 Emerson came most fully under the influence of Neoplatonism, while at the same time he was enlarging his knowledge of the Orient. In 1841 he was reading Proclus, Porphyry, Iamblichus, Hermes Trismegistus, Synesius, and others — all in Thomas Taylor's translations; and was confiding to his Journals his most enthusiastic praise of the "Trismegisti" or "Platonists". That July he took three new volumes of Taylor's translations with him on a trip to Nantasket while preparing his address on "The Method of Nature". In 1842–43 he again was reading many of Taylor's volumes. And during these years he made many entries in his Journals on the Neoplatonists, showing especial admiration for the newly discovered Proclus. In 1843 a striking passage on this philosopher occurs, preceded by remarks on "Ward's Chinese Book", and followed closely by passages on "Woman", the "true sex" of minds, and Buddhism.[1] — Here, as often, the juxtaposition of subjects is suggestive; and China, Neoplatonism, Buddhism, and the feminine principle are seen

[1] *Journals*, VI, 374–382.

to be related in the course of Emerson's mental development.

But Emerson's interest in Neoplatonism did not cease after this sudden outburst in the early 40's; rather it continued steadily to the end of his life, even more markedly than did his interest in the Orient. Plotinus, Proclus, and Iamblichus are mentioned frequently in his later years, along with the Persian poets, and some Hindu philosophy. Porphyry is listed in 1870, Iamblichus in '71, Saadi, the Zend Avesta, and a Hindu poem in '72, while finally in '74 Plotinus is listed — the last philosopher to be mentioned in Emerson's Journals.[1]

Thus it is evident how, beginning about eight years after Emerson's reading of Neoplatonism, his reading of Oriental books began. It followed closely upon his interest in Neoplatonism, the one developing naturally out of the other, and continuing along with it. And so, although in many text books the Neoplatonists are described as "Platonists" and Greeks, for the present pur-

[1] In the later volumes of *Journals*, the editors have omitted many European writers from mention in Emerson's reading lists, fearing monotonous repetition; and so these lists are not conclusive evidence. However, the actual text of the *Journals* proves the importance of Neoplatonism, and these reading lists at least prove the relative importance of Neoplatonism as compared with Orientalism in Emerson's reading.

poses they may be treated as Orientals — both because of the affinity of their philosophy to that of the Orient, and because they were of prime importance in introducing Emerson to Oriental thought.

The sources from which Emerson's interest in Neoplatonism sprang are interesting, because again they are often the same as the sources of his Orientalism. He found both Neoplatonism and Orientalism described in the Cyclopedia of De Gérando, which he read so carefully. Later, in 1837, he copied into his Journals a long passage from Plotinus which he had found quoted in Goethe. And Goethe was probably responsible for his acquaintance with the Persian poets — Hafiz especially. Finally, Emerson's Neoplatonism and his Orientalism were both encouraged by his friendship with the chief members of the Transcendental movement. It is significant that his more intense interest in Neoplatonism occurs at about the same time as Bronson Alcott's visit to England, and his acquaintance with Messrs. Wright and Lane, two English mystics. The library of these Englishmen, containing many of Thomas Taylor's translations and some Oriental works as well, was brought to America by its owners during the year 1842 or earlier.[1] And these books stimulated the interest in mysticism among the Transcendentalists. Finally, it is interesting that the majority of the copies of Thomas Taylor's translations acquired by the Harvard University Library are dated "1843", at this same time. — Thus, in the early 1840's, Neoplatonism was attracting the interest of the "literati" of Greater Boston. We may also remember that not long after this Thoreau received a shipment of Oriental books from England, and that these eventually passed into Emerson's hands, and were read by him in his later years.

Finally, in tracing the relation of Neoplatonism and of Orientalism in Emerson's thought, and in indicating the importance of Neoplatonism, a tabulation of the frequency with which each Neoplatonist is mentioned in the annual reading lists may help, even if artificially, to show their relative values, to Emerson. As a standard of comparison, we may note that Hafiz, the Oriental writer whom Emerson read most frequently, is mentioned during fourteen different years — although, as a poet, he provided literature of a much less severe type than did the

[1] Clara E. Sears, *Bronson Alcott's Fruitlands* (New York, 1915), p. 181 ff.

obscure philosophers of Alexandria. Among these, Plotinus was read during 18 different years, first in 1830, and last in 1874. The name of Proclus is mentioned during 12 years; Iamblichus 8; Porphyry 7; Synesius 6; while the works of the other Neoplatonists attracted Emerson's interest less frequently.

It is clear that Emerson read these Neoplatonists constantly during his mature life. A later discussion will attempt to show how they influenced his thinking. Though he did not begin reading them until comparatively late in life, his first published work, *Nature*, was not written until he was thirty-three years old, and even this shows clear evidence of his reading of the Neoplatonists. They helped him to formulate his philosophy. They inclined his mind toward an interest in the Orient. And yet it is a remarkable fact that none of the standard biographies and critical studies show any clear appreciation of their importance to Emerson.

Emerson's first biographer, Oliver Wendell Holmes, mentions the Neoplatonists only once, in treating the Over-Soul essay. He writes: "It is a curious amusement to trace many of these thoughts and expressions to Plato, or Plotinus, or Proclus, or Porphyry; to Spinoza, or Schelling."[1] And Mr. O. W. Firkins, in his biography, states: "The two qualities of strongest appeal were the religious strain which he found in the various Bibles, in Plato, in Plotinus, in Herbert; and the strain of racy vigor... in Montaigne."[2] Even Mr. G. E. Woodberry, who was perhaps in the best position to appreciate Emerson's true debt to Neoplatonism (through his scholarly relations with Mr. John S. Harrison, the exponent of Emerson's Neoplatonism), has made only the following short explanation: "Hafiz is in his poetry what Plotinus is in his prose, a far horizon line, which helps to give that suggestion of eternity to his thought, of universality to his truth, which characterize his writing."[3] — These remarks are all pertinent, but incomplete and incidental only.

This comparative neglect of Neoplatonism as a prime factor in influencing Emerson's intellectual development may be due to various causes. Perhaps the chief is that the Neoplatonists are seldom mentioned by name in Emerson's published *Works*. For Emerson their philosophy

[1] O. W. Holmes, *Ralph Waldo Emerson* (Boston, 1884), p. 173.

[2] O. W. Firkins, *Ralph Waldo Emerson* (Boston, 1915), p. 231.

[3] G. E. Woodberry, *Ralph Waldo Emerson* (New York, 1907), p. 168.

was so elemental and abstract that he naturally absorbed it to himself, without specific quotation, or mention of the sources from which he drew. But secondly, to modern readers, Neoplatonism itself is so cold and abstruse, that it is not apt to attract them. It repels the average investigator. And when it does not repel, it fascinates him — which is often worse. Mr. John S. Harrison, the only scholarly investigator who has fully dealt with the subject, has ascribed far too great an importance to it, and has gone beyond the limits of safe criticism.

THOMAS TAYLOR

The uncritical quality which Neoplatonism engenders, is emphasized by the literary personality and style of Thomas Taylor, its first English translator. Taylor is perhaps typical of all Neoplatonism, for he, more than any man, was wholeheartedly fascinated by it. He was a strange mixture of recluse, and scholarly enthusiast. Characterized by the elder Disraeli as "a modern Pletho", he was fabled to have sacrificed a bull to Jupiter. Plato, and the ancients possessed his allegiance. He harbored scorn for all modern civilization, and lived in proud poverty all his life. At his death he left behind him between sixty and seventy volumes of Latin and Greek translations.

These translations form his chief claim to fame. They were largely of Plato, Aristotle, and the Neoplatonists. He considered not only the Neoplatonists, but also Aristotle, as "in the strictest sense the holders of the Platonic dogmas, contrary to the ignorant and rash deductions of the moderns." [1] But even these translations are of untrustworthy scholarship, and their phraseology is crabbed and obscure. Coleridge described them as "difficult Greek translated into incomprehensible English." [2] And they had but little currency in the England of Taylor's day. Taylor, however, avenged himself on his unfriendly and unappreciative public by outbursts such as the following, which he included in his Introduction to Aristotle: "The period in which it was begun and finished, is Barren; the country in which it is published, Commercial; and the enemies of it are *the worst of men*, but its friend is Divinity." [3]

It was this scholar-recluse who at once provided Emerson with the Neoplatonist writings

[1] *The Platonist* (Osceola, Mo.), II, 71.

[2] J. D. Campbell, *Samuel Taylor Coleridge* (London, 1896), p. 13, n.

[3] *The Platonist*, I, 150.

that he so loved, misguided him by his identification of Plato and the Neoplatonists, and repelled many other literary men and philosophers by his fanaticism and by the crabbed style of his translations. Indeed, he and his translations have been so seldom praised, and withal are so odd and unpromising, that the high regard in which Emerson held them is remarkable. It indicates how eager he was to accept and praise anyone who helped him to the reading of his favorite Neoplatonists.

But the fact is undeniable. Emerson has left many sentences to testify to his admiration for Taylor. In his essay on "Poetry and Imagination" he wrote: "There are also prose poets. Thomas Taylor, the Platonist, for instance is really a better man of imagination, a better poet, or perhaps I should say a better feeder to a poet, than any man between Milton and Wordsworth." This is strong — almost extravagant — language. But it is repeated in *English Traits*, where Emerson recounted a conversation with Wordsworth: "I told him it was not creditable that no-one in all the country knew anything of Thomas Taylor, the Platonist, whilst in every American library his translations are found."[1] And still again, in his essay on

[1] *Works*, V, 295.

"Plato", Emerson lists Taylor as one of the "Platonists" of all time: "How many great men Nature is incessantly sending up out of the night to be *his men* — Platonists! The Alexandrians, a constellation of genius... Sir Thomas More, Henry More, John Hales, John Smith, Lord Bacon, Jeremy Taylor, Ralph Cudworth, Sydenham, Thomas Taylor; Marcilius Ficinus and Picus Mirandola." Certainly an odd, and a significant list! And in another passage Emerson mentions Thomas Taylor in the same breath with the "Platonists of Oxford".[1]

Many unofficial statements by Emerson also bear witness to his high opinion of Taylor. "Mr. Emerson spoke of him (Thomas Taylor) as a Greek born out of time, and dropped on the ridicule of a blind and frivolous age."[2] And again, speaking of his English visit, Emerson had said: "Thomas Taylor, the Platonist, is totally unknown in England... I asked repeatedly among literary men for some account of him. But in vain. Poor Taylor in his day had insulted over the materialism and superstition of the times... And the modern multitude, which he despised, avenged themselves by forgetting him."[3] Finally, in an article printed after Emer-

[1] *Works*, V, 224. [2] *Ibid.*, VII, 409, note. [3] *Ibid.*, V, 40.

son's death, an auditor wrote up some notes he had taken at one of Emerson's later lectures, quoting him as saying: — "Thomas Taylor was a man of singular character: a rugged Englishman without one refreshing stroke of wit, or even of good sense; haughtily believing in his work, he accepted poverty proudly to the end of its accomplishment... Taylor received scorn for scorn. Even learned England knew nothing of him, gave him no attention. Hallam had never heard of him, nor Millman, nor, I think, Macaulay."[1] — In these last quotations it is clear that Emerson was not blind to Taylor's faults. But on the whole he admired and praised Taylor more than any other great writer has done, before or since.

EMERSON ON THE NEOPLATONISTS

This enthusiasm which Emerson showed for Thomas Taylor is significant chiefly because it parallels the enthusiasm which he showed for the Neoplatonist philosophers whom Taylor translated. His expressions concerning them show as much admiration, and as little dispraise. His words are seldom ambiguous.

In his First Series of Essays, Emerson wrote of

[1] *Atlantic Monthly* (June, 1883), LI, 827.

> that lofty and sequestered class...the Trismegisti, the expounders of the principles of thought from age to age. When at long intervals we turn over their abstruse pages, wonderful seems the calm and grand air of these few, these great spiritual lords who have walked in the world... This band of grandees, Hermes, Heraclitus, Empedocles, Plato, Plotinus, Olimpiodorus, Proclus, Synesius, and the rest, have somewhat so vast in their logic, so primary in their thinking that it seems antecedent to all ordinary distinctions... With the geometry of sunbeams the soul lays the foundations of Nature. The truth and grandeur of their thought is proved by its scope and applicability... But what marks its elevation and has even a comic look for us, is the innocent serenity with which these babe-like Jupiters sit in their clouds, and from age to age prattle to each other and to no contemporary. Well assured that their speech is intelligible, and the most natural thing in the world, they add thesis to thesis, without a moment's heed of the universal astonishment of the human race below, who do not comprehend their plainest argument.[1]

This is an impressive, but also a well-considered burst of eloquence.

But it may be objected that in the above passage, Emerson merely treats of the Neoplatonists as members of a "sequestered class", in which he includes the greatest Greek thinkers also. And also, Emerson says: "when, at long intervals, we turn their pages." Yet it has

[1] *Works*, II, 345–7.

already been seen how constantly Emerson returned to the pages of Plotinus and Proclus. And, if we examine his Journals, we find that he was inspired to the above outburst by a specific reading of Plotinus. — In his Journals he wrote: "Wonderful seemed to me, as I read Plotinus, the calm and grand air of these few..." [1]

And Emerson's specific remarks on the different Neoplatonists are still more convincing. His high appreciation of Proclus is recorded at frequent intervals. In 1842 he wrote: "Such a sense dwells in these purple deeps of Proclus transforms every page into a slab of marble, and the book seems monumental. They suggest what magnificent dreams and projects. They show what literature should be." [2] And later he again exclaimed: "When I read Proclus, I am astonished with the vigor and breadth of his performance. Here is... an Atlantic strength which is everywhere equal to itself and dares great attempts, because of the life with which it feels itself filled." [3] The next year he noted: "I read Proclus for my opium" — and this has been cited by Mr. Edward Emerson and others as a statement of dispraise. But the quotation should be read in full:

[1] *Journals*, V, 510. [2] *Ibid.*, VI, 159. [3] *Ibid.*, VI, 205.

By all these and so many rare and brave words I am filled with hilarity and spring, my heart dances, my sight is quickened, I behold shining relations between all beings, and am impelled to write and almost to sing. I think one would grow handsome who read Proclus much and well.... But this inebriation I spoke of... is inspiration.

This is further proved by the continued interest in Proclus which Emerson showed. In 1845 he wrote: "*Proclus*. I... do not think he has his equal among contemporary writers."[1] In 1847, he again exalted him.[2] And he continued to cite him in later years.

Emerson also had high praise for the lesser Neoplatonists. In his essay on "Books" he speaks of "*Providence*, by Synesius, translated into English by Thomas Taylor... one of the majestic remains of literature." In the same passage he quotes the praise of Emperor Julian on Iamblichus, that "he was posterior to Plato in time, not in genius." And late in life, Emerson confided to his Journals: "I remember I expected a revival in the churches to be caused by reading Jamblichus."[3]

As against these, a few passages from the Journals may be cited to show Emerson in a mood of revulsion from Neoplatonism. But

[1] *Journals*, VII, 7. [2] *Ibid.*, VII, 262. [3] *Ibid.*, IX, 88.

these are few, and they do not bulk large against the passages of endorsement. They follow: "Platonists: a decline into ornament from the severity of strength. — Corinthian, Byzantine. Plato is grand; they are grandiose."[1] And again: "With what security and common sense this Plato treads the cliffs and pinnacles of Parnassus, as if he walked in a street, and came down again into a street as if he lived there. My dazzling friends of Alexandria, the New Platonists, have none of this air of facts and society about them."[2] But the passage most often cited to show the qualifications of Emerson's Neoplatonism is from his essay "Nominalist and Realist". Again, as in the "opium" passage, the whole text should be given:

> I find the most pleasure in reading a book in the manner least flattering to the author. I read Proclus, and sometimes Plato, as I might read a dictionary, for a mechanical help to the fancy and the imagination. I read for lustres... 'Tis not Proclus, but a piece of nature and fate that I explore. It is a greater joy to see the author's author than himself. A higher pleasure of the same kind I found lately at a concert, where I went to hear Handel's Messiah.

Dispraise of the Neoplatonists is rare: and twice, at least, words of Emerson's which have

[1] *Journals*, VII, 96. [2] *Works*, IV, 310, n.

been quoted in dispraise, actually express an individual and discriminating sort of praise.

This may perhaps be most clearly seen in the juxtaposition of two striking passages from Emerson's *Works*. These passages show an unconscious admiration for Neoplatonism, and are all the more convincing because they are not preconsidered. In his volume on *Nature*, Emerson had stated that "A wise writer will feel that the ends of study and composition are best answered by announcing undiscovered regions of thought, and so communicating, through hope, new activity to the torpid spirit." [1] Later, in his essay on "Books", he spoke of the Neoplatonists in the same words, saying: "The reader of these books makes new acquaintance with his own mind; new regions of thought are opened." — At times the Neoplatonists assumed an almost Messianic significance to Emerson. And a sentence from the Journals gives further confirmation to the striking coincidence of phrase which has just been noticed: "When I read Plato or Proclus," Emerson wrote, "or ascend to thought, I am apprised of my vicinity to a new and bright region of life." [2] Or, as he wrote later: "This [is] most stimulating philo-

[1] *Works*, I, 70. [2] *Journals*, VI, 199.

sophy."[1] Emerson read the Neoplatonists not for opium, but for inspiration.

PLOTINUS

It is interesting that in all these passages where Emerson praises Neoplatonism, Plotinus has seldom been mentioned. And yet it was Plotinus whom Emerson admired most, and who most influenced him. The reason for this silence is clearly that he took the greatness of Plotinus for granted, and so expressed less of the enthusiasm of spiritual discovery when writing of him. Often he lists him among the great thinkers of all time. One of these is especially interesting because it occurs in a description of his "revered aunt", Mary Moody Emerson. Of her he said: "Plato, Aristotle, Plotinus — how venerable and organic as Nature they are in her mind."[2] And Plotinus was mentioned and quoted often in the correspondence between aunt and nephew.

But perhaps the most impressive allusion which Emerson makes to Plotinus is in the "Song of Nature", where he couples him with Jesus, Shakspeare, and Plato as one of the most perfect men Nature has produced:

[1] *Journals*, VII, 8.

[2] *The Atlantic Monthly* (Dec. 1883), p. 734.

Twice I have moulded an image
  And thrice outstretched my hand,
Made one of day and one of night
  And one of the salt sea-sand.

One in a Judaean manger,
  And one by Avon stream,
One over against the mouths of Nile,
  And one in the Academe.

With Plotinus we pass from the external statements which Emerson made concerning the Neoplatonists to a discussion of the internal evidence of the influence of Neoplatonism to be found in his published *Works*. The evidence is not far to seek. To the first edition of Emerson's first published work, *Nature*, he prefixed a motto from Plotinus: "Nature is but an image or imitation of wisdom, the last thing of the soul; Nature being a thing which doth only do, but not know." At the outset of Emerson's writing there occurs this striking quotation. And, although in second and later editions this motto was omitted, some verses of Emerson's own being substituted, the evidence remains, and justifies further search in Emerson's writing for traces of Neoplatonism.

But, passing over the six volumes which form the center of Emerson's life work, the spiritual influence of Plotinus may again be seen at the end of his writings as it was at the beginning. The final paragraph of his essay on "Illusions", the last essay of the volume on *The Conduct of Life*, has been called a "magnificent epilogue" to his writing. It describes the experience of the young mortal in the hall of the firmament. It is of great beauty, and although it has often been quoted, it may be given again:

> There is no chance and no anarchy in the universe. The young mortal enters the hall of the firmament; there is *he alone with them alone*, they pouring on him benedictions and gifts, and beckoning him up to their thrones. On the instant and incessantly, fall snow-storms of illusions. He fancies himself in a vast crowd which sways this way and that, and whose movements, and whose doings he must obey... What is he that he should resist their will, and think or act for himself? Every moment new changes and new showers of deceptions to baffle and distract him. And when, by and by, for an instant, the air clears and the clouds lift a little, there are the gods still sitting around him on their thrones, — *they alone with him alone*.[1]

The notes to the Centenary Edition suggest the influence of a passage from the *Phaedo* of Plato on the thought and imagery of this passage. But the influence of Plotinus is also clear. For at the very end of the *Select Works of*

[1] *Works*, VI, 325. The italics are added.

Plotinus, Taylor has thus translated his author:

> This, therefore, is the life of the Gods, and of divine and happy men; a liberation from all terrene concerns, a life unaccompanied with human pleasures, and *a flight of the alone to the alone.*

Thus amid the high poetic beauty of Emerson's late essay there is twice employed the poignant phrase of Plotinus: "the alone to the alone". It is harmonized with the rich Platonic symbolism of the description; and it echoes through the passage like the tolling of a distant bell: "they alone with him alone", repeating a variation on the previous phrase: "he alone with them alone". It adds the lonely exaltation of Plotinus to the imaginative symbolism of Plato. It furnishes the crown of Emerson's writing. It shows the spiritual influence of Plotinus repeated at the end as it had been prefixed at the beginning. And to dispel any doubt of this echoing, the phrase is quoted by Emerson in his earlier essay on "Swedenborg", to describe the mystic experience: "'the flight', Plotinus called it, 'of the alone to the alone.'"

Plotinus is typical of Neoplatonism. The beginning and end of Emerson's life work may be taken as typical of the central part of it. Further evidences of Neoplatonism scattered through his pages have already been collected by Mr. J. S. Harrison, in *The Teachers of Emerson*, and the specialist will find valuable material there. But for the more general purposes of this discussion, Emerson's own explicit statements, and the striking evidence cited above must suffice to prove the importance of Neoplatonism. The philosophic ideas which Emerson derived — in part, at least — from Neoplatonism, will be considered in the next chapter.

CHAPTER IV

NEOPLATONISM

"That lofty and sequestered class...the Trismegisti, the expounders of the principles of thought..."

— EMERSON'S *Works*, II, 345.

MANY of Emerson's chief philosophic ideas correspond strikingly to those of Neoplatonism, and some may be traced directly to that philosophy. Since *Nature* has been said to contain most of Emerson's philosophy in miniature, and since it was his first published work, an investigation of the Neoplatonic ideas in it may be of especial interest. But since most of Emerson's reading in the Neoplatonists was of a later date, their effect on his more mature philosophic ideas can be clearly seen only in his later essays. Indeed, at the time of writing *Nature*, Emerson had not yet come on Taylor's translations of the Neoplatonists. All phrases in it suggestive of Neoplatonism seem to be derived indirectly, from secondary sources. And yet many Neoplatonic borrowings occur.

The first motto to *Nature* was from Plotinus. Yet it was derived indirectly from a quotation from Plotinus in Ralph Cudworth's *True Intellectual System of the Universe*, as Mr. Harrison has pointed out.[1] The second and present motto, however, obviously composed in later years, concludes as follows:

> And, striving to be man, the worm
> Mounts through all the spires of form.

And this motto also seems related to the philosophy of Plotinus, who had expressed the idea more abstractly:

> If, previously to a serious inquiry into nature, we should...affirm that all things desire contemplation, and verge to this as their end, not only rational animals but those destitute of reason; likewise that... some things pursue contemplation differently from others, some in reality, and some by imitation...; shall we not appear to advance a doctrine entirely new?[2]

The worm, an animal "destitute of reason", may aspire "by imitation", to the typical virtue of man, namely, contemplation, and "verges to this as its end". — Of course this is only a vague parallel of idea, and yet in both Emerson and Plotinus, the idea is discussed "previously to a serious inquiry into nature". Emerson may have derived his suggestion from the general

[1] *The Teachers of Emerson*, p. 34.

[2] Thomas Taylor, *Five Books of Plotinus*, pp. 199–200.

evolutionary doctrines then in the air. Yet the parallel with Plotinus is interesting and suggestive, even if not conclusive.

The presence of the influence of Plotinus in the first, and perhaps in the second motto to *Nature* might indicate that Emerson took his larger theory of Nature from Neoplatonism. But of the eight chapters which constitute *Nature*, two seem to show especial relation to that philosophy.

The first of these deals with "Nature as Language". It describes the symbolic or poetic aspect of things. Nature, by means of concrete illustrations, suggests the ideal meaning of the world. This is closely related to Emerson's theory of poetry, which, as will be seen later, is almost entirely Neoplatonic. The doctrine is most concisely stated as follows:

> The world is emblematic. Parts of speech are metaphors, because the whole of nature is a metaphor of the human mind. The laws of moral nature answer to those of matter as face to face in a glass. "The visible world and the relation of its parts, is the dial plate of the invisible". The axioms of physics translate the law of ethics.

This doctrine, which would identify the laws of Nature with the laws of the Soul — which would discover, as Emerson later expressed it, "the analogy that marries Matter and Mind" — is related to Neoplatonism. The Neoplatonists held that Nature was merely the material counterpart of the divine order. Again we remember Emerson's sentence describing the Neoplatonists: "With the geometry of sunbeams the soul lays the foundations of Nature. The truth and grandeur of their thought is proved by its scope and applicability."[1] Professor Woodbridge Riley, in his *History of American Thought*, also notices the Neoplatonic source of this idea, stating: "That the axioms of physics apply to morals is not of the Academy, but of a later school, being rather of Plotinus than Plato."[2]

In general, then, the belief that Nature is "language" — that every natural object has a meaning which transcends the natural world, and that the laws of Nature apply also to the world of the soul — is Neoplatonic. Two specific sentences in this section of *Nature* confirm this view. Near the beginning, Emerson states: "Spirit is the Creator. Spirit hath life in itself. And man in all ages and countries embodies it in his language as the FATHER." The use of "the Father" as a synonym for "spirit", is common

[1] *Works*, II, 346. [2] p. 166.

in the terminology of Neoplatonism, and in a later essay on poetry, Emerson quotes one of Taylor's "Chaldaean Oracles", that "Poets are standing transporters, whose employment consists in speaking to the Father and to matter."[1]

Later, near the end of the section on "Nature as Language", Emerson borrows a sentence from Neoplatonism. He writes: "This relation between the mind and matter is not fancied by some poet, but stands in the will of God, and so is free to be known by all men. It appears to men or it does not appear." This last phrase is directly borrowed from Plotinus, who, describing the mystic experience, writes: "It either appears to us, or it does not appear." It is interesting that in this case Emerson borrowed the Neoplatonic quotation through the medium of Coleridge, and again did not find it in Thomas Taylor's translations.[2]

The other chapter of *Nature* which is strongly tinged with Neoplatonism is the final one entitled "Prospects". In this the statement occurs that a wise writer will do best "by announcing undiscovered regions of thought" — and we have seen that Emerson said of the Neoplatonists: "New regions of thought are opened." But

[1] *Works*, VIII, 19. [2] See *The Teachers of Emerson*, p. 298.

immediately after this sentence Emerson continues: "I shall therefore conclude this essay with some traditions of man and nature, which a certain poet sang to me." And, after several pages of poetic prophecy, ascribed to this unknown poet, he concludes: "Thus my Orphic poet sang."

This brings up the much discussed question of the identity of Emerson's Orphic poet.— Who was he, and how were these strange prophecies suggested? The question cannot be answered finally, but the general tone of the prophecies is the same as that of Neoplatonic mysticism. They begin: "The foundations of man are not in matter, but in spirit." This sentence alone suggests an affinity to Neoplatonism. And the prophecies continue with strange myths concerning the world.

In the notes of the Centenary Edition, the following illuminating passage from Proclus is cited: "He who desires to signify divine concerns through symbols is orphic, and, in short, accords with those who write myths concerning the Gods." And Mr. Harrison has argued that Emerson, working from this suggestion, composed the prophetic passage himself.[1] But

[1] *The Teachers of Emerson*, p. 246.

Emerson had surely not read Proclus at this time, and probably did not know of his doctrine of the Orphic. Again it has been suggested that Emerson was inspired to compose the passage by a conversation with his Transcendental friend, Bronson Alcott. This is possible, for Alcott was deeply versed in Neoplatonism—especially in the fabulous aspects of it.

No one, however, has ever suggested the possibility—rather the probability—that originally Emerson's Orphic poet was, in very truth, an Orphic poet—or a sort of synthetic Orphic poet at the most. When Emerson was in college, "Orphic remains" were a subject for lectures, and we have his own testimony on the subject in his Journals for September, 1842. Here he describes his old teacher Edward Everett, as lecturing to "green boys from Connecticut, New Hampshire and Massachusetts... on the Orphic and ante-Homeric remains. This learning instantly took the highest place to our imagination in our unoccupied American Parnassus."—In all probability, Emerson's "Orphic poet" is Emerson himself, paraphrasing and elaborating passages of the Orphic remains as described by Edward Everett and others at Harvard College. Inasmuch as Neoplatonism set great store by

Orphism, and took over much of the oracular material of that ancient religion, it is probable that in the case of the "Orphic poet", Emerson derived his Neoplatonism from one of its own original sources.

In the concluding paragraph of *Nature*, Emerson again quotes "his poet" as saying: "Nature is not fixed, but fluid. Spirit alters, moulds, makes it. The immobility or bruteness of nature is the absence of spirit; to pure spirit it is fluid, it is volatile, it is obedient. Every spirit builds itself a house, and beyond its house a world, and beyond its world a heaven. Know then that the world exists for you." Here the Neoplatonism is clear. Emerson, in his peroration, is expounding the Neoplatonic doctrine that matter is the absence of spirit, and that to spirit all is possible. He is, in this last passage, developing Neoplatonism so that it shall lead into Emersonianism, shall "open undiscovered regions of thought, and communicate, through hope, new activity to the torpid spirit".

Thus Emerson's first published work, *Nature*, shows strong suggestions of his Neoplatonic reading. Most of these suggestions came to him indirectly, for not till 1838 did he come on Taylor's translations of the Neoplatonists. Yet he took his first motto to *Nature*, indirectly, from Plotinus. His second motto, self-composed, is similar to a passage from Plotinus. His section that deals with "Nature as Language," is full of Neoplatonic thought. And the final section sets forth the Neoplatonic idea that the immobility of Nature is due to the apparent absence of the divine spirit, from which all the world has emanated. He uses this doctrine to suggest how man, by the reassertion of his spiritual powers, may remould Nature nearer to the divine, and may build his own world.

THE OVER-SOUL

If Emerson's discussion of *Nature* is often Neoplatonic, — his doctrine of the Over-Soul practically *is* Neoplatonism. It is the theory of spiritual emanation — the theory that, from an Absolute source, the living water (or sometimes the metaphor is that of light) streams down into all creatures below, imparting to them the divine vital energy.

A short passage of Plotinus will illustrate the common metaphor: "That which subsists above life is the cause of life.... Conceive, then, a fountain possessing no other principle, but imparting itself to all rivers, without being exhausted by any of them, and abiding quietly in itself."[1] Compare this with the language of the "Over-Soul" essay: "When I watch that flowing river, which, out of regions I see not, pours for a season its streams into me, I see that I am a pensioner; not a cause but a surprised spectator of this ethereal water; that I desire and look up and put myself in the attitude of reception, but from some alien energy the visions come." Later, Emerson uses the metaphor of the spiritual light: "By the same fire, vital, consecrating, celestial, which burns until it shall dissolve all things into the waves and surges of an ocean of light, we see and know each other, and what spirit each is of."

Again in the "Over-Soul" essay Emerson treats of "*Revelation*", and describes it in the language of Neoplatonism. "For this communication is an influx of the divine mind into our mind. It is an ebb of the individual rivulet before the flowing surges of the sea of life." And in this same paragraph he lists: "The trances of Socrates, the 'union' of Plotinus, the vision of Porphyry", and others, as examples of the influx of the divine mind.

At the end of the essay, Emerson expresses the Neoplatonic idea (which we have already

[1] Thomas Taylor, *Five Books of Plotinus*, p. 237.

noticed in *Nature*) of the parallelism which exists between Nature and Spirit, between the Individual and the Absolute. And in this passage there seems to echo something of the exalted loneliness of Plotinus:

> The soul gives itself, alone, original and pure, to the Lonely, Original and Pure, who, on that condition, gladly inhabits, leads and speaks through it. Then it is glad, young and nimble.... Behold, it saith, I am born unto the great, the universal mind. I, the imperfect, adore my own Perfect. I am somehow receptive of the great soul...

Finally, the question of the source of the title, "Over-Soul", comes up. It has several times been suggested[1] that Emerson got the phrase from the Hindu term "Adhyâtman" — "adhi" meaning "above" or "superior", and "atman" meaning "soul" — which occurs in the Bhagavat Gîta. But a survey of Emerson's reading shows that he had not read the Bhagavat Gîta in 1841 when the "Over-Soul" essay was published. And so the term must be declared original to Emerson, who had only such phrases as "World Soul" and "Universal Soul" of Neoplatonism to help him. This source of suggestion seems suffi-

[1] W. T. Harris, in *The Genius and Character of Emerson*, ed. by F. B. Sanborn; and also J. S. Harrison, *The Teachers of Emerson*, p. 277.

cient, however, just as the Neoplatonic conception underlying it seems sufficient to account for the central idea of Emerson's essay.

THE THREE PLANES

It has been seen how Emerson, in all his writing contrasted Nature and Spirit, and suggested the close relation between the two. He considered Nature as parallel to Spirit — as symbolizing the higher reality. In general terms this is what Neoplatonism taught. But dialectically Neoplatonism felt the necessity of explaining more in detail the age-old problem of the parallelism between Nature and Spirit — the interrelation between mind and matter. This it did in various ways. Poetically, by the use of fable, it described a daemonic realm as existing between the Celestial and the Natural. Daemons thus became the mediators between supernatural "gods", and human beings — between pure Spirit, and Nature. Daemonology, of minor importance in Plotinus, treated allegorically in Plato, came to be typical of all Neoplatonism in its later exponent, Iamblichus, who composed a treatise on "Daemonology". According to him there were three planes of being — the Celestial, the Daemonic, and the Natural. There were gods, demi-gods, and men. Obviously it was this fabulous idea which Emerson developed in his poem "Initial, Daemonic and Celestial Love". But this poem was suggested originally by a passage from Plato, and so may be passed over here.[1]

Plotinus, however, dealt with the need of mediation between Spirit and Nature more rationally. He described three gradations between the world of Spirit and the world of Nature — three distinct planes of being. These are known as the hypostases of Plotinus. As Dean Inge expounds: "There are two fundamental triads in Plotinus. One of these is the trinity of Divine principles — the Absolute (τὸ ἕν,) spirit, (νοῦς), and soul (ψυχή); the other is the tripartite division of man into Spirit, Soul, and Body. This triadic schematism was becoming almost obligatory for a Greek philosopher."[2]

Emerson took over the general idea that man may live on any of three different planes of being, but he did not keep the strict formalism of the triads of Plotinus. In general he designated these planes of being as first, the "intellectual",

[1] For a complete discussion of this, see *The Teachers of Emerson*, pp. 146–57.

[2] W. R. Inge, *The Philosophy of Plotinus*, I, 122.

second, a middle region variously described, and third, the "material" or "sensuous". He changed his terminology constantly and, what is more, he varied his emphasis on these three as his philosophy matured.

The growth of this concept in Emerson's mind is interesting, and his change of emphasis on the various planes of being is highly significant. In his early years he wrote an apotheosis of Thought:

> Better it is than gems of gold
> And oh! it cannot die,
> But thought will glow when the sun grows cold
> And mix with deity.[1]

He considered the intellectual life the highest. And in *Nature* Emerson still kept much of his reverence for thought — for the unassisted intellect. Here, however, his term "Spirit" probably is meant to include both the intellectual and the moral life of man, in contrast to the Natural, or sensuous.

But in his later essay on the "Over-Soul" the three planes of being are clearly distinguished, and the emphasis changes. Or rather, the emphasis disappears, and the three are conceived as coequal. Emerson writes: "When it [the Over-

[1] *Works*, IX, 380.

Soul] breathes through his intellect, it is genius; when it breathes through his will, it is virtue; when it flows through his affection, it is love. And the blindness of the intellect begins when it would do something of itself."

Finally, in the second series of essays, Emerson's reverence for thought turns to depreciation. His essay on "Experience" is extreme in its statements, and yet it marks the trend of his mind. In it he writes:

> What help from thought? Life is not dialectics. ...The great gifts are not got by analysis. Everything good is on the highway. The middle region of our being is the temperate zone. We may climb into the thin and cold realm of pure geometry and lifeless science, or sink into that of sensation. Between these extremes is the equator of life, of thought, of spirit, of poetry, — a narrow belt.

Here, it may be noted, "thought" and "spirit" are included also in the middle region of life, but the emphasis has changed. No longer is pure intellect deified. No longer are the abstractions of Neoplatonism the realm of "the geometry of sunbeams" — exalted. Later in the essay Emerson again clearly affirms that "The mid-world is best." And in his later years he never qualified that statement, nor gave such great emphasis to the intellectual world.

Thus Emerson, even when he was following a suggestion of Neoplatonism in his classification of the levels of human life, did not abide by the conclusions of that philosophy. He changed his allegiance from the world of pure thought to that of experience. And this change of allegiance is not only significant for the understanding of Emerson, but for the understanding of modern thought, as well. For, starting from Emerson, certain modern writers have made the distinction between the "super-rational", the "rational", and the "sub-rational" levels of life; and the emphasis has usually been placed on the super-rational, — the realm of the exalted intellect. In the mature Emerson the emphasis was on the normal, rational man, in opposition both to the intellectualism of the Neoplatonic philosophy, from which this doctrine of the planes of being was derived, and to modern intellectualist critics, who have taken the idea over from Emerson.

EVIL AS NEGATION

In his theory that evil is merely the absence of good Emerson gave expression to still another doctrine of Neoplatonism, — a doctrine which has usually been considered peculiar to that philosophy. Yet it lies implicit in the theory of Nature which Emerson and Neoplatonism held in common, and is also related to Oriental thought. If, as Emerson wrote, "the immobility or bruteness of nature is the absence of spirit"; then evil and the bruteness of man must be due to the same cause. If matter is the absence of spirit, evil is the absence of good. So Neoplatonism taught, and Emerson also.

Among the Neoplatonists Proclus wrote a treatise "On The Subsistence of Evil". In it he asserted: "There is not such a thing as unmingled evil... form or essence of evil.... For evil is nothing else than a greater or less declination, departure, defect and privation from *the good itself*... in the same manner as darkness from the sun."[1]

It is clearly with this passage in mind that Emerson asserted, in his essay on "Experience", that: "Sin, seen from the thought, is a diminution, or *less*.... The intellect names it shade, absence of light, and no essence." — Here the parallelism of phrase and idea reveals Emerson writing with the specific passage of Proclus in mind. Indeed, his Journals at this time show that he had just been reading Proclus. And in

[1] *The Six Books of Proclus On the Theology of Plato*, II, 500.

his poetic motto prefixed to this essay on "Experience", he further suggested the Neoplatonic doctrine of evil by listing "spectral Wrong" as one of the apparent "Lords of Life".

In Emerson's earlier writing, also, the idea that evil is merely the absence of good is clearly expressed. It is most strikingly set forth in his address to the Harvard Divinity students, delivered in 1838. At this time he had not yet come on Proclus, but was for the first time making the acquaintance of other Neoplatonists in Thomas Taylor's translations. These writers helped him to clarify his doctrine. He wrote:

> Good is positive. Evil is merely privative, not absolute: it is like cold, which is the privation of heat. All evil is so much death or nonentity.... Whilst a man seeks good ends, he is strong with the whole strength of nature. In so far as he roves from these ends, he bereaves himself of power, of auxiliaries; his being shrinks out of all remote channels, he becomes less and less, a mote, a point, until absolute badness is absolute death.[1]

This whole doctrine is implicit in the Neoplatonic theory of the bruteness of Nature—which is expressed partly in Plotinus. Dean Inge expounds: "There are unquestionably passages in which Plotinus seems to make matter

[1] *Works*, I, 124.

the principle of evil. Side by side with such expressions as 'absence of good'; 'deprivation', 'absolute poverty', we find that matter is 'the first evil.'"[1]

In the philosophy of Plotinus Emerson found the theory of Nature, and the theory of Evil, joined. And in his final section of *Nature* (where we have already noticed the signs of Neoplatonic influence), he also partially associated these theories. He describes Nature as "a great shadow pointing always to the sun behind us". And later he asserts: "The ruin or the blank that we see when we look at nature, is in our own eye. The axis of vision is not coincident with the axis of things, and so they appear not transparent but opaque." And again we quote Dean Inge on Plotinus: "Matter intrudes where it has no right to be. It obscures the light which shines upon the soul, by mingling its own darkness with it."[2]

Thus, tracing back Emerson's doctrine of evil to its source, we see how he clarified it as he read more and more in the Neoplatonists. In *Nature*, he had hardly developed it at all. It is only implicit in the doctrine of the bruteness of

[1] W. R. Inge, *The Philosophy of Plotinus*, I, 134.

[2] *Ibid.*, I, 131.

matter, which he does express clearly. Two years later, when he first was reading Taylor's Neoplatonic translations, he clearly expressed the doctrine that evil is the absence of good, in his Divinity School Address. And in 1844, after reading Proclus, he made his most specific references to the doctrine in his essay on "Experience", and gave it final form.

ART AND "THE POET"

Finally, in Emerson's theory of Art, and Poetry, he is most clearly developing a concept which he found uniquely in the writings of the Neoplatonists. — In *Nature*, he had drawn several of his ideas from Neoplatonism; but through secondary sources. In his essay on the "Over-Soul" he dealt with the fundamental idea of Neoplatonism; but in general terms. In his doctrine of the three planes of being he developed a suggestion which he found in Neoplatonism; but turned it to his own uses. In his theory of evil he adopted a purely Neoplatonic idea; and yet he never mentioned or quoted the Neoplatonists in describing it. But in his theory of poetry he not only developed a concept which he had found in Neoplatonism; but he also copied a long and significant passage from Plotinus on "Art" into his Journals, and quoted from almost all the Neoplatonists in his Essays in order to clarify the doctrine.

Plotinus differed most strikingly from Plato on this theory. Plato taught that Art is merely imitative. It is an imitation of Nature, which is in turn the imitation of the ideal. A statue merely imitates a man, who in turn is an individual and imperfect imitation of the ideal man. Thus, to Plato, Art is at a third remove from reality, and is unworthy of praise. But Plotinus believed otherwise, and Emerson quoted a passage from him in his Journals for 1837. This contradicts Plato as follows:

> But would any one despise Art because it imitates Nature? Let us reply, that the natures also imitate many others; that, moreover, Art does not directly imitate that which the eyes can see, but goes back upon the Rational out of which Nature consists, and after which Nature worketh.
>
> ... So could Phidias form the God, although he imitated nothing perceptible to the senses, but made, himself in his mind, such a form as Jove himself would appear if he should become obvious to our eyes.[1]

— Plotinus believed that Art may imitate the ideal directly, and so may achieve equality with Nature. But only equality, for Art, like

[1] *Journals*, IV, 220–1.

Nature, must make use of matter, and so cannot achieve ideal perfection. Plotinus illustrated this concept with the following parable, which Emerson duly copied into his Journals:

> Let two stone blocks be placed together whereof one is rough and without artificial labor, but the other is formed by art to a human or divine statue.... To you will the stone which is brought by art into a beautiful form appear altogether beautiful, yet not because it is stone, since then will the other block also pass for beautiful, but because it has a form which art has imparted to it.
>
> But matter has no such form; but this was in the thinker before it came to the stone.... [The form] does not abide pure in itself, nor quite as the artist wishes, but only as far as the material would obey Art.... Therefore must the workman be more excellent than the work.[1]

The artist, by virtue of his mind, may conceive of the ideal form, although he may not impart it perfectly to the material of his work. But even the artist may not conceive of this abstract ideal unless he be open to the influence of the divine mind — the Over-Soul. The artist must be inspired in order that his conception may be a true one. In his essay on "The Poet" Emerson writes of this inspiration: "The poet knows that he speaks adequately then only

[1] *Journals*, IV, 219–20.

when he speaks somewhat wildly, or, 'with the flower of the mind',... or as the ancients were wont to express themselves, not with the intellect alone, but with the intellect inebriated by nectar." And even here Emerson is quoting phrases which Plotinus had used in describing the mystic experience — "with the flower of intellect", and "intellect intoxicated with nectar". [1]

Thus, from Plotinus came all the ideas necessary to Emerson's theory of Art: — ideal imitation, the equality of Art and Nature, and inspiration from the Over-Soul. With them in mind it is more easy to understand Emerson's poem, "The Problem", which expresses this theory most concisely:

> The hand that moulded Peter's dome
> And groined the aisles of Christian Rome
> Wrought in a sad sincerity;
> Himself from God he could not free;
> . . . .
> For out of Thought's interior sphere
> These wonders rose to upper air
> And Nature gladly gave them place,
> Adopted them into her race
> And granted them an equal date
> With Andes and with Ararat.
> These temples grew as grows the grass;
> Art might obey but not surpass.

[1] Plotinus, *Select Works*, p. 477; and *On Suicide*, p. 98. (See *The Teachers of Emerson*, 211–2.)

— The artist, inspired by the divine mind, may create works of equal value with the works of Nature, but may not surpass her.

Most of the theories which Emerson developed from Neoplatonism lay implicit in his first book on *Nature*. And so his doctrine of "Nature as Language" is at the basis of this theory of poetry. In his first book he tells how Nature, with her "divine visual language", continually speaks to man of the divine or ideal world. And although Art may seem to speak more intelligibly to man, because of having been already translated, as it were, into his dialect, Art and Nature are actually coequal. To the inspired poet or artist, all Nature is language.

This theory is most fully developed in Emerson's essay on "The Poet". Here he quotes Proclus twice, and Iamblichus, and constantly echoes phrases from Plotinus while developing his theme. When he was composing the essay, in 1841, he wrote to his friend, Elizabeth Hoar: "I have also three volumes new to me of Thomas Taylor's translations, Proclus, Ocellus Lucanus, and Pythagorean Fragments." And throughout the essay itself there is an overtone of Neoplatonic thought and phraseology, to which Mr. Edward Emerson has called attention in his Notes.

A few of these phrases may be strung together to illustrate the trend of thought in this essay. Emerson writes: "Let us, with new hope, observe how nature... has insured the poet's fidelity to his office of announcement and affirming.... Nature offers all her creatures to him as a picture-language. 'Things more beautiful than every image', writes Iamblichus, 'are expressed through images.' Things admit of being used as symbols because nature is a symbol, in the whole, and in every part." — This is much like the language which we have noticed in "Nature", but here Iamblichus is quoted, and the Neoplatonism is more marked.

On the next page Emerson expands his idea as follows, and quotes Proclus: "The Universe is the externalization of the soul.... 'The mighty heaven', said Proclus, 'exhibits, in its transfigurations, clear images of the splendor of intellectual perceptions; being moved in conjunction with the unapparent periods of intellectual natures.'... Since every thing in nature answers to a moral power, if any phenomenon remains brute and dark it is because the corresponding faculty in the observer is not yet active." — Here Emerson is developing the passage of Proclus; and, considering the barbarous language in which he found Proclus translated, we may affirm that he did well not to quote further from the text of the Neoplatonist.

Later Emerson uses an illustration from Plotinus: "The world being thus put under the mind for verb and noun, the poet is he who can articulate it.... As the eyes of Lyncaeus were said to see through the earth, so the poet turns the world to glass, and shows us all things in their right series and procession." But this fable of Lyncaeus had been previously expressed by Plotinus: "It [i.e. the world] appears as a part; but by him whose sight is acute, it will be seen as a whole; *viz.*, by him whose sight resembles that which Lyncaeus is said to have possessed, and which penetrated the interior of the earth; the fable obscurely indicating the acuteness of the vision of supernal eyes."[1] And soon after this passage Emerson uses the phrases of Plotinus already noted: "with the flower of the mind", and "intellect inebriated by nectar".

Later still, in this same essay, "Orpheus" and "Proclus" are cited in succession to illustrate the power of good similes, or "tropes"; as "when Orpheus speaks of Hoariness as 'that white flower which marks extreme old age'; when

[1] *Select Works of Plotinus*, "Introduction", p. lxxxi.

Proclus calls the universe the statue of the intellect."

Finally, it is especially interesting that in the last sentence of the peroration of this essay on "The Poet", Emerson draws his language from Persian Poetry — so that again we see Neoplatonism and Orientalism existing side by side. Emerson concludes to his poet: "and, though thou shouldst walk the world over, you shalt not be able to find a position inopportune or ignoble." And in his Journals for 1841, he had noted: "Hafiz defies you to show him or put him in a condition inopportune and ignoble." [1]

Clearly, Emerson's poetic theory is developed from that of Plotinus, and his essay on "The Poet", especially, is full of Neoplatonisms. But the other works in which he dealt with poetry and beauty also contain suggestions of the same sort; as when, in his later essay on "Beauty", he quoted Proclus, that "Beauty swims on the light of forms." In an earlier "Ode to Beauty", he addressed Beauty in the same phrase:

Thee gliding through the sea of form
Like the lightning through the storm.

While his poems "Woodnotes", and "The

[1] *Journals*, V, 562.

Poet", contain the same sort of reminiscences of Neoplatonism.[1]

Perhaps this theory of poetry may be said to illustrate Emerson's intellectual liking for Neoplatonism better than any of the other theories which he developed from that philosophy. For he first shadowed forth this theory in *Nature*. It is central to his thinking, being related to the Over-Soul doctrine also. It is clearly not derived from Plato, and is the theory on which Emerson most directly quoted all the Neoplatonists. It is the theory which he develops most frequently in his essays and poems. And yet, perhaps, it is the theory which seems most particularly transcendental, and most "Emersonian" — in the extreme sense of the word.

NEOPLATONISM, TRANSCENDENTALISM, AND GERMAN IDEALISM

This is probably because of the close intellectual relationship existing between Neoplatonism and the Transcendental school of thought. This relationship has not been fully recognized, partly because Transcendentalism has usually been considered as a literary movement, and its precursors as poets and men of

[1] See Mr. Edward Emerson's *Notes* to these poems.

letters, rather than as philosophers. So in his paper on "Life and Letters in New England", Emerson wrote of the Transcendentalists that "Perhaps they only agreed in having fallen on Coleridge and Wordsworth and Goethe, then on Carlyle, with pleasure and sympathy."[1] But Coleridge had helped introduce Emerson to Plotinus, and from the point of view of philosophy, at least, the Neoplatonists could be called the precursors of Transcendentalism. This is especially true of the most intellectual members of the Transcendental group — Alcott and Emerson — who read the Neoplatonists very extensively.

It has often been said that the German philosophers, especially Kant, were, philosophically, the precursors of Transcendentalism. Transcendentalism has sometimes even been described as the American manifestation of the thought of Kant and Schelling and Hegel. But in the case of Emerson, at least, the facts do not bear this out. In Emerson's *Works*, Kant is only mentioned twice — one reference being merely incidental. In Emerson's Journals he is only discussed twice — being described as a "technical analyst".[2] And of the rest of the German

[1] *Works*, X, 342. [2] *Journals*, V, 306.

philosophers there is almost as little mention. Hegel is not discussed in Emerson's Journals till 1846, and then is referred to at second hand, through a description by Cousin. Indeed, Schelling is the only German idealist whom Emerson read at all widely; and he never referred even to Schelling with any unusual enthusiasm.

The investigation of the relative importance of the Germans and the Neoplatonists to Transcendentalism emphasizes the power which a mere name can exert. Emerson, in his much-quoted lecture on "The Transcendentalist", ascribed the origin of the term "Transcendental" to Kant, saying: "It is well known to most of my audience that the Idealism of the present day acquired the name Transcendental from the use of the term by Immanuel Kant, of Königsberg,... The extraordinary profoundness and precision of that man's thinking has given vogue to his nomenclature, in Europe and America, to that extent that whatever belongs to the class of intuitive thought is popularly called at the present day Transcendental." But this statement applies only to the name "Transcendental", and not to the movement itself, nor to the source of its philosophic theories. Actually Coleridge initiated the Transcendentalists to

Neoplatonism, and Neoplatonism furnished them with several of their philosophic ideas. The development of the German school was in large measure parallel to Transcendentalism, and separate from it. A statement made by Emerson when, late in life, he was reading Hegel, is interesting. — "Hegel", he wrote, "pre-exists in Proclus."[1] Indeed, the importance of Neoplatonism — as shown by Emerson's reading lists, his enthusiastic statements of admiration for it, and his use of Neoplatonic ideas — is so great, and has been so little recognized in the past, that there is much danger of its being over-emphasized now.

There are several doctrines which Emerson found in Neoplatonism, but which were more strikingly developed in Oriental literature. Chief of these is that which lies behind the poem "Brahma" — the idea of the absolute unity of the creative energy of life. Of this Mr. Harrison writes: "The sentiment of the third stanza:

> They reckon ill who leave me out;
> When me they fly, I am the wings;
> I am the doubter and the doubt,
> And I the hymn the Brahmin sings —

is that teaching familiar in Greek philosophy

[1] *Works*, VIII, 180.

from Parmenides through Plato to the Neoplatonists; namely that the knower and the thing known are one; or, as the poem says — 'I am the doubter and the doubt'.[1]" Yet, if any idea, or any poem, was ever "derived" from any literary source, the idea and expression of "Brahma" was derived purely from the *Bhagavat Gîta* and the *Katha Upanishad*. Emerson may have found the vague foreshadowing of this idea in the Neoplatonists and Plato; but the form and the spirit of it he derived from Hindu literature.

Similar to this, but much less clear as to its derivation, is the idea lying behind Emerson's essay on "Illusions". In this essay occur phrases and ideas reminiscent both of Plato, the Neoplatonists, and of the Orient; but the predominant tone of the essay is Oriental. And an examination of Emerson's Journals at the time of writing the essay shows that the Hindu conception of "Maya" controlled the spirit of his writing; although Platonism and Neoplatonism had prepared his mind for the Hindu thought.[2]

[1] *The Teachers of Emerson*, p. 278. *Vide infra*, Chapter V, also.

[2] *Vide infra*, Chapter V, for a more complete discussion of this.

Emerson almost never used Neoplatonic thought exclusively, in the development of his ideas. Not the Neoplatonists, nor yet the Platonists, were "*the* teachers of Emerson". And so, if this present discussion has focused its attention unduly on Neoplatonism, and has conveyed the impression that Emerson derived his major inspiration from the Neoplatonists, it is only necessary to gain the proper perspective again by glancing through Emerson's annual reading lists, and by noting the great bulk and variety of his reading in the more modern Western literatures. Neoplatonic books formed an important, but a small fraction of his reading. And further, even though Emerson was discovering Neoplatonism at the same time that he was composing his first two series of essays, the titles and substance of these essays are significant. For, although "The Over-Soul" and "The Poet" contain much Neoplatonic thought, "Self-Reliance" and "Compensation", "Friendship", and "Manners" — to take only the best known — contain little or none.

The significance of Neoplatonism to Emerson's philosophy may perhaps best be limited under three heads. First, it furnished a background of vague "transcendental" thought,

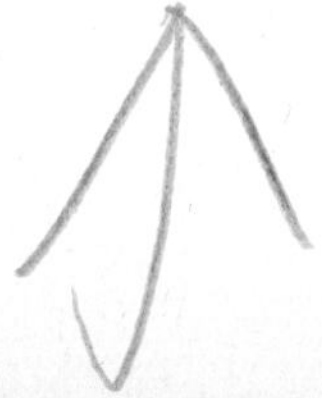

which, superadded to the poetic thought of Coleridge and Wordsworth and Goethe, formed the most distinctive element of Transcendentalism. Second, it suggested to Emerson certain philosophic ideas and conceptions which he developed and expressed in his subsequent essays and poems. Third, it prepared Emerson's mind (and to a lesser extent, Alcott's and Thoreau's) for the Oriental translations which were to influence the later thinking of these men. Neoplatonism was not all-important to Emerson's thinking. It merely stood at the crossroads where Eastern and Western thought met. Emerson, although always a far-traveler, spent most of his life on the highways of Western thought.

LUSTRES

Yet all generalizations are dangerous. Just as Transcendentalism was more than a philosophic idealism, so Neoplatonism was more than a mere system of thought. Neoplatonism was volatile, even when its specific doctrines seemed hard, and it reappears strikingly in many new forms and places. We have tried to show that some of its specific doctrines were developed by Emerson. But he himself maintained that he read the Neoplatonists chiefly for suggestion and stimulation — "for lustres", as he expressed it. Even in the distorted translations of Thomas Taylor he found nuggets of true wisdom. So some of the best of these, which he incorporated into his Journals during his random reading, may be quoted in conclusion, as illustrating the more attractive side of Neoplatonism. These are some of the "lustres", not generally known or reprinted. Emerson noted:

Let me say with Plotinus: "Since therefore you admire the soul in another thing, admire yourself."

Plotinus: Where does the light come from? — From the soul of the sufferer and of the enjoyer.

Porphyry: Life is that which holds matter together.

Proclus: Will is the measure of Power.

Plotinus: Dance. Under the soul of the world, "the bodies are moved in a beautiful manner, as being parts of the whole: but certain things are corrupted, in consequence of not being able to sustain the order of the whole. Just as if, in a great dance, which is being conducted in a becoming manner, a tortoise being caught in the middle of the progression should be trod upon, not being able to escape the order of the dance; though, if the tortoise had arranged itself with the dance, it would not have suffered from those that composed it."[1]

[1] Compare this with the conception of Havelock Ellis, in *The Dance of Life*. Ellis also had read Plotinus.

Proclus: Why fear to die? At death the world receives its own.

Iamblichus: Dissolvers of Fate.

— Of such stuff, then, was Neoplatonism.[1]

[1] For a list of the Neoplatonic books which Emerson probably read, see J. S. Harrison, *The Teachers of Emerson*, especially the Bibliography.

CHAPTER V

THE WISDOM OF THE BRAHMINS

Then I discovered the Secret of the World; that all things subsist, and do not die, but only retire a little from sight and afterwards return again.

— EMERSON'S *Journals* for 1844.

TO Emerson's mind Hindu philosophy expressed the essence of Orientalism. Often he identified the whole Orient with it. When speaking vaguely of "Asia", he was usually thinking of Hindustan. Even Persia, with its wealth of poetry, occupied only a secondary position for him, and in his essay on "Persian Poetry" he carefully limited his statements with the proviso that he was "leaving out of view, at present, the genius of the Hindoos (more Oriental in every sense), whom no people have surpassed in the grandeur of their ethical statement."

The first Oriental translation that Emerson read was a fragment of Hindu verse: "To Narayena"; and at this same age of 19 he wrote to his Aunt that he was curious to read "your Hindu mythologies, the treasures of the Brahmins." From this time on these treasures beckoned on his Eastern horizon, and the more he knew of them, the more valuable they proved. His reading of Indian literature forms one of the most important chapters in the story of his literary development; for not only did he owe his poems "Brahma" and "Hamatreya" entirely to Hindu works, but large parts of his essays on "Plato", "Fate", "Illusions", and "Immortality" are based on Hindu thought, and his famous "Sphinx" probably shares in it. It is significant that these works of Emerson's — like all those that derived partly from his Oriental reading, belong to the latter half of his literary career.

As we have seen, his first published works gave slight evidence of Oriental reading. What evidence there is, however, points to Hindu literature — and "Viasa" is the only Oriental name to appear in his first *Nature*. Later, in reading Colebrooke's essays, he must have found out that Viasa was only the fabulous title for the unknown compilers both of the *Vedas* and of the *Mahabharata* — the great Indian epic.[1] And even so, Emerson had listed Viasa

[1] See H. T. Colebrooke, *Miscellaneous Essays* (London, 1837), I, 10.

along with Berkeley as a philosopher — not as a poet or man of religion.

By 1841, in the *Essays, First Series*, Emerson wrote with more information of the theory of the transmigration of souls, in his "History" essay. This constitutes the only clearly Oriental idea in this volume, and it will be seen that he came on even this idea in a book of Platonism. In his various essays produced between 1841 and 1844, when the *Essays, Second Series* were published, Indian quotations are the chief Oriental ones, and they are only four in number, all referring to Buddhist sayings, and probably all taken from the same source.[1]

Thus, although Indian influence is slight in Emerson's published writing through 1844, it is more plentiful than that of any other Oriental nation. Emerson's Journals, and the annual reading lists compiled from them, illustrate the growth of his interest in Hindu literature more fully.

His first Journal references to India or to Hindu books are of a general nature, and have already been noticed. — First they evidenced enthusiastic anticipation; then a doubt and distrust arising from the disparaging accounts that

[1] See *Works* I, 337; III, 163, and 236; XII, 395.

he had read in such places as the *Edinburgh Review*; and then a total lack of interest. In 1830, among his notes from De Gérando, is listed "The *Mahabarat*, one of the sacred books of India", but with little amplification of the note. And no further entries occur till "Vyasa" in 1834, in the list of his reading for that year.[1] How unimportant this entry is, we have already seen.

In 1836, the year of the publication of *Nature*, Emerson seems first to have read a definite book of Indian translated literature, as the "Code of Menu" is listed among his reading for that year. However, this title disappears from the list in 1837. In 1838 it reappears, along with the general title "Buddha". — Evidently at this time he was becoming seriously interested in the new material. In '39 and '40 the "Vedas" are listed, and in '40 "Buddha" reappears. Also in '40 the first actual quotation from any of these books appears in his Journals, on "Buddhist hospitality".[2] In '41, '42, and '43 the "Veeshnu Sarma" or "Heetopades" is mentioned. In '44 there is nothing; and finally in 1845 the "Bhaga-

[1] Complete abstracts from these reading-lists are to be found reprinted in tabular form in the Appendix.

[2] *Journals*, V, 408.

vat-Geeta", "Vishnu Purana", and "Colebrooke's *Essays*" all appear for the first time, together with several other titles, repeated.

In some cases, however, the Journals seem not to give the earliest mention of Emerson's reading of certain books. For instance in 1840, in a letter, he speaks of "The Vedas, the bible of the tropics, which I find I come back upon every three or four years."[1] Since his first Journal mention of this work occurred in 1839, only the year previous, there seems to be a discrepancy. Probably either Emerson's informal statement partook of what he called "oriental largeness", or else he had read selections from the Vedas before then, without listing them specifically in his Journals. It may well be that the mention of "Vyasa" in the reading-lists of 1834, referred to selections from the Vedas.

In another letter, written in 1843 to Miss Elizabeth Hoar, he states that "The only other event is the arrival in Concord of the Bhagavat Gita, the much renowned book of Buddhism [!], extracts from which I have often admired, but never before held the book in my hands."[2] Again, this date is two years in advance of men-

[1] *Letters of Emerson to a Friend* (Boston, 1899), p. 27.

[2] D. L. Maulsby, *Emerson* (Tufts College, 1911), p. 122.

tion in the Journals — seeming to indicate that the latter were not always kept up to date. Finally, Emerson wrote a short introduction to extracts from the "Veeshnoo Sarma" in *The Dial* for 1842, which is not mentioned elsewhere.

Thus, gathering the evidence together, we find that probably Emerson had read no complete book of Hindu literature before 1836, when he finished *Nature*, which has been said to contain all of his philosophic ideas in miniature. Between 1836 and 1845 he read the following five Indian translations: (1) The "Code of Menu", (2) "Buddha", (3) The "Vedas", (4) "Veeshnu Sarma", and perhaps (5) the "Bhagavat Gita". The "Code of Menu", first read of the five, never affected his thinking much, even in later years. He published selections from the "Veeshnu Sarma" in *The Dial.* But only from one of these five books ("Buddha") did he quote in his own writings, either Journals or Essays, before 1845.

This book on "Buddha", then, was the only one which clearly affected Emerson's writing before that date. After it, however, many and various quotations throng both his Journals and *Works*. In 1845, a passage from the Vishnu Purana inspired his poem "Hamatreya". At the same time another passage from the same work sowed the germ of what was later to become the poem "Brahma". And during that year passages from the *Bhagavat Gîta*, from the Vedas (*per* Colebrooke's *Essays*), and from "Buddha" were copied, to be incorporated later in the *Representative Men* volume.

This volume of biographical essays, we have seen, contains a wealth of Oriental material. In it, the specifically Hindu thought is often fused with the general Oriental material, to which it dictates the tone, and of which it is the most significant. After the "Plato" essay, the Hindu material becomes interwoven so completely with Emerson's own thought that, except for a few specific poems, it may best be noticed under the head of the different ideas of Emerson's to which it related itself.

Some of the specific Hindu books in which Emerson was most interested may, however, be mentioned separately. For instance, the *Bhagavat Gîta*, which he first saw in 1843, was still of current interest in 1849, when he wrote to H. G. O. Blake, saying: "Perhaps you will send me in a day or two some hint of your experiences in the Bhagavat Geeta, that will be a text, and will find me in better leisure."[1] During this same period, the *Vishnu Purana* was stimulating Emerson's mind, and, though less generally known, seems equally as important to Emerson as the *Bhagavat Gîta*. In 1847, Emerson copied in his Journals the following passage under the heading "*Orientalist*. Says Goethe, 'The English translator of the Cloud-Messenger, Megadhuta, is likewise worthy of all honour, since the first acquaintance with such a work always makes an epoch in our life'."[2] In 1856, Emerson's first reading of the *Katha-Upanishad* led directly to his writing of "Brahma". Finally, in 1862, on the death of Thoreau, Emerson received by bequest from his friend's library about twenty volumes[3] of Hindu literature, which he read in later intervals. These tomes are still to be seen standing imposingly on the bottom shelf of Emerson's library in Concord. They bear witness to the importance of Hindu literature to his mature writing.

"BRAHMA"

Emerson's poem "Brahma" probably expresses the central idea of Hindu philosophy

[1] *Journal of English and Germanic Philology*, XXVI, 481.
[2] *Journals*, VII, 291–2. [3] See Appendix for these titles.

more clearly and concisely than any other writing in the English language — perhaps better than any writing in Hindu literature itself. A Hindu scholar, writing recently in an American journal, quotes with approval the opinion of Professor Lanman of Harvard, that

> The doctrine of the absolute unity finds perhaps its most striking expression in Sanskrit in the Katha-Upanishad, but nowhere, neither in Sanskrit nor in English, has it been presented with more vigor, truthfulness, and beauty of form than by Emerson in his famous lines paraphrasing the Sanskrit passage.[1]

And other students of Hindu literature have expressed themselves to the same intent.

But "Brahma" is not only one of the finest expressions of the Hindu idea of absolute unity, it is one of Emerson's own best poems, and represents on Emerson's part a deep and subtle reworking of the Hindu idea. It stands at the end of a series of poems and essays, and exemplifies in itself Emerson's ability to work with this foreign material at his best. It was not something which he casually wrote off after reading some Hindu book, although he tried to do something of the sort, at first. It was not the product

[1] *Harvard Theological Review*, IV, 411. Article by Herambachandra Maitra.

of any one day, or any one passage of Hindu literature. It had been taking shape over the long period of Emerson's reading of Hindu translations, and it was finally composed in 1856 — comparatively late in his life.

Since the poem is intrinsically so excellent, and since it is typical of Emerson's methods of treating Oriental material, a close study of it proves valuable. Especially is this true, in that all the facts concerning the genesis and growth of the poem are available. The result may help to show not only how Emerson dealt with Oriental sources, but how his creative mind worked at its best — making a new and perfect poem out of old snatches of a foreign idea.

The materials for this reconstruction have in part been gathered before,[1] but not all of them have been discovered, and they have never been assembled in one place. If this reconstruction were entirely possible, the result should approximate, on a small scale, that achieved so perfectly by Professor J. L. Lowes in his study of *The Road to Xanadu*. The story of "Brahma" describes the road travelled by Emerson to ancient Hindustan.

[1] See *Journals*, IX, 56; *Works*, IX, 464–66; F. B. Sanborn, ed., *The Genius and Character of Emerson*, pp. 372–77; and D. L. Maulsby, *Emerson*, pp. 123–25.

For purposes of convenience, the poem may be reproduced here:

If the red slayer think he slays
Or if the slain think he is slain,
They know not well the subtle ways
I keep, and pass, and turn again.

Far or forgot to me is near;
Shadow and sunlight are the same;
The vanished gods to me appear;
And one to me are shame and fame.

They reckon ill who leave me out;
When me they fly, I am the wings;
I am the doubter and the doubt,
And I the hymn the Brahmin sings.

The strong gods pine for my abode,
And pine in vain the sacred Seven;
But thou, meek lover of the good!
Find me, and turn thy back on heaven.

The subject is the absolute unity of the world — of man and nature — under the various illusions or external appearances of things. In the poem, "Brahma" — the impersonal creative force of the world, is represented as the speaker. The idea may perhaps be related to the modern concept of the conservation of energy, which declares that no electron is ever lost in the universe, no matter where it goes, or what form it assumes. From the point of view of the electron — of the energizing force — of Brahma, nothing ever dies, because the energy in the thing merely changes form when the body apparently dies.

This idea first presented itself to Emerson in its full force in 1844, when, after reading some Oriental book,[1] he wrote in his Journal: "Then I discovered the Secret of the World; that all things subsist, and do not die, but only retire a little from sight and afterwards return again." Of course this "Secret of the World" is merely the vague, unformulated idea of "Brahma".

The definite suggestion of "Brahma" as a poem came to Emerson in 1845, when he copied into his Journal a passage that he had just read in the *Vishnu Purana*: "What living creature slays or is slain? What living creature preserves or is preserved? Each is his own destroyer, as he follows evil or good." And soon he versified the thought as follows:

> What creature slayeth or is slain?
> What creature saves or saved is?
> His life will either lose or gain,
> As he shall follow harm or bliss.[2]

Here the first two lines of "Brahma" are foreshadowed, although the subsequent verses are entirely different. At about this same time he

[1] The entry occurs immediately after another Oriental notation. *Journals*, VI, 494.

[2] *Journals* VII, 127; and *Works* IX, 465.

was also reading the *Bhagavat Gîta*, and in it he must have seen a passage bearing on the same idea more explicitly: "The man who believeth that it is the soul which killeth, and he who thinketh that the soul may be destroyed, are both alike deceived; for it neither killeth, nor is it killed."[1]

Meanwhile, in his essay on "Plato", in 1850, he expressed this same idea in prose, adapting the passage from his Journals of an earlier date:

> In all nations there are minds which incline to dwell in the conception of the fundamental Unity.... This tendency finds its highest expression in the religious writings of the East, and chiefly in the Indian Scriptures, in the Vedas, the Bhagavat Geeta, and the Vishnu Purana. Those writings contain little else than this idea, and they rise to pure and sublime strains in celebrating it.
>
> The Same, the Same: friend and foe are of one stuff; the ploughman, the plough and the furrow are of one stuff; and the stuff is such and so much that the variations of form are unimportant.... "What is the great end of all, you shall now learn from me. It is soul, — one in all bodies, pervading, uniform, perfect, preeminent over nature, exempt from birth, growth and decay,... The knowledge that this spirit, which is essentially one, is in one's own, and in all other bodies, is the wisdom of one who knows the unity of things."[2]

[1] Chapter II, verse 18. Emerson was using the translation of Sir Charles Wilkins, 1785.

[2] *Works*, IV, 49–50.

Here the idea of "Brahma" is explained by Emerson a little more at length, and in a rather cramped prose, very much like that of the translations that he was reading.

Finally, in 1856, eleven years after his first reading of the *Vishnu Purana* passage, Emerson was reading the *Katha Upanishad* (the source to which Professor Lanman ascribes the whole of "Brahma"); and here he came upon the following passage, which, along with other passages from the same book, seems to have given him the necessary impetus to compose "Brahma" much as it now stands: "If the slayer thinks that I slay, or if the slain thinks I am slain, then both of them do not know well. It (the soul) does not slay, nor is it slain."[1] But by this time he had become so familiar with the thought that he no longer copied the passage into his Journals. The only way we can be sure that he read it for this third time is that he copied other passages from this same translation of the *Upanishad* into his Journals along with "Brahma", which he evidently composed then. These other passages furnished some of the thought for the later verses of his poem. But many of its verses seem

[1] Emerson was probably reading the translation by E. Roer, *Biblioteca Indica*, vol. XV (Calcutta, 1853), p. 105.

to have been suggested more particularly by passages from the *Bhagavat Gîta* and the *Vishnu Purana.* A close line-by-line comparison of the poem with its probable sources shows how Emerson's mind used and transmuted his material, and how he retained many of the ideas in his mind over a long period of time.

The first two lines, as we have seen, have their source in all three of the Hindu books. Lines 3 and 4: "they know not well the subtle ways, I keep..." may be paralleled to the phrases of the *Katha Upanishad*: "they do not know well", and "the soul being more subtle than what is subtle".[1] (We must remember that the "I" of the poem is the same as "the soul" of the *Upanishad.*)

In the second stanza, line 5: "Far or forgot to me is near", may be related to "He is far, and also near".[2] And likewise lines 6 and 7: "Shadow and sunlight are the same; The vanished gods not less appear", may be related to the same source: "From whom the sun rises and in whom it sets again, him all the gods entered".[3] But finally line 8: "And one to me are shame and fame" finds no parallel in the *Upanishad*, but

[1] *Upanishad*, p. 105; copied in *Journals*, IX, 57.

[2] *Ibid.* [3] *Ibid.*, from the *Upanishad*, p. 111.

only in the *Bhagavat Gîta*, which Emerson had read many years earlier: "He... to whom praise and blame are alike".[1]

Of the third stanza, lines 9, 10 and 11: "They reckon ill who leave me out; When me they fly, I am the wings; I am the doubter and the doubt" seem to have no direct parallel. The thought only is to be found in the following lines copied by Emerson from the *Upanishad*: "He proceeds from death to death who beholds here difference.", and "There is no doubt concerning it [the soul]". While again the last line of the stanza: "And I the hymn the Brahmin sings", is again to be paralleled only to the *Bhagavat Gîta*: "I am the sacred verse".[2]

In the final stanza Mr. W. T. Harris has identified "the strong gods" as Indra, god of the storm; Agni, god of fire, and Yama, god of death, who "are absorbed into Brahma at the close of the Kalpa;" [3] and the "sacred Seven" as the seven "Maharshis," or highest saints. Finally, the last, striking line of the poem: "Find me, and turn thy back on heaven," is paralleled vaguely in the *Bhagavat Gîta* [4] by: "The high-

[1] *Bhagavat Gita*, Chapter XII, verse 19. [2] Chapter IX, 19.
[3] F. B. Sanborn, ed. *The Genius and Character of Emerson*, p. 377.
[4] Chap. VIII, 17.

souled ones, who achieve the highest perfection, attaining to me, do not again come to life... All worlds, O Arguna! up to the world of Brahman, are destined to return. But... after attaining to me, there is no birth again." And yet perhaps a closer parallel is to be found in Emerson's own earlier writing: "That which the soul seeks is resolution into being above form, out of Tartarus and out of heaven, — liberation from nature" — a passage which occurs in his essay on "Plato".

Thus the poem "Brahma," perfectly adapted and expressed as it is in the verse of Emerson, is fundamentally composed of an ancient idea, the parts of which were absorbed at various times from the Hindu scriptures. This idea had been present in Emerson's mind for many years before "Brahma" was composed, and much of it had meanwhile been expressed in prose by Emerson himself in his earlier essay on "Plato".

Indeed, Emerson expressed this idea for a third time at the close of his later essay on "Immortality," writing: "Brahma the supreme, whoever knows him obtains whatever he wishes. The soul is not born; it does not die; it was not produced from anyone. Nor was any produced from it. Unborn, eternal, it is not slain, though the body is slain, subtler than what is subtle, greater than what is great..."

This idea of "Brahma" was clearly a favorite one with Emerson. In its simplest terms it is — as Emerson had written in "Plato": "the conception of the fundamental unity... — friend and foe are of one stuff; the ploughman, the plough and the furrow are of one stuff." This conception he obviously derived from the Hindu books which he was reading at this time. But just as clearly, this conception lay latent in his essay on the "Over-Soul", which he had written before reading any of the three Hindu books in question. There he had said:

> Meantime within man is the soul of the whole; the wise silence; the universal beauty, to which every part and particle is equally related; the eternal ONE. And this deep power in which we exist and whose beatitude is all accessible to us, is not only self-sufficing and perfect in every hour, but the act of seeing and the thing seen, the seer and the spectacle, the subject and the object are one.

This is the theory of the Over-Soul, and this contains also the germ of "Brahma": friend and foe, subject and object, alike partake of the divine energy — of the Over-Soul. The conception, as Emerson developed it in the "Over-Soul" essay, however, had its sources in Neoplatonism. In "Brahma" it derived from Hinduism. The history of this idea furnishes perhaps the best example of the importance of observing the sequence of Emerson's reading and thought. The "Over-Soul" idea has been termed "Hindu", and the "Brahma" idea has been termed "Platonic" — in a sense each statement is true; yet Emerson advanced through Neoplatonism to Orientalism, and the one explained, supplemented, and enriched the other within his mind.

It has been suggested[1] that Emerson may have taken the title for his "Over-Soul" from the *Bhagavat Gîta*, where the Supreme Spirit is called *adhyatman*, or "the superior soul". But Emerson had not read this Hindu book at the time of writing the "Over-Soul", and although he had read "extracts" from it before, it is doubtful if the term can be claimed to be of Hindu origin. The question of the relative importance of Orientalism and of Neoplatonism is impossible of final determination, and can only be answered at all by studying the progress of

[1] By W. T. Harris in *The Genius and Character of Emerson*, ed. F. B. Sanborn; and by John S. Harrison, *op. cit.*, p. 277.

Emerson's reading and thought at the periods when he was writing his various essays.

"HAMATREYA" AND "ILLUSIONS"

Toward the end of his life, Emerson quoted in his Journals two Hindu words meaning "Over-Soul". In doing so, he indicated the connection between the idea of the "Over-Soul", (of "Brahma"), and that of "Illusions", (and of his poem "Hamatreya"). He conceives of Brahma as the supreme unifying force of the world — the source of all energy — the Over-Soul. Illusions, personified by the Hindu goddess, Maia, give the appearance of variety to the world. Maia is the creatress of the individual soul of man. And so Emerson wrote in his notebook called *Orientalist* that there was

> In the history of intellect no more important fact than the Hindoo theology, teaching that the beatitudes or Supreme Good is to be obtained through science; namely, by perception of the real and the unreal, setting aside matter, and qualities and affections or emotions and persons and actions as *Maias* or illusions, and thus arriving at the contemplation of the one Eternal Life and Cause and a perpetual approach and assimilation to Him; thus escaping new births and transmigration.
>
> The highest object of their religion was to restore that bond by which their own self (atman) was linked

to the Eternal *Self* (paramatman) [i.e. Over-Soul]; to recover that unity which had been clouded and obscured by the magical illusions of reality, by the so-called Maia of Creation.[1]

Here we see that the idea of Maia — namely, that there are "magical illusions of reality" — is really the negative of the "Over-Soul" idea, and of "Brahma". Just as the latter is comparable to the Platonic "unity"; so Emerson's Oriental conception of "Illusions" is comparable to the Platonic "variety", or the "flowing". "Brahma" and "Illusions" are the positive and negative of the same idea. And so Emerson coupled them in his "Plato" essay, part of which has already been quoted:

"You are fit" (says the supreme Krishna to the sage) "to apprehend that you are not distinct from me. That which I am, thou art, and that also is this world, with its gods and heroes and mankind. Men contemplate distinctions because they are stupefied with ignorance." "The words *I* and *mine* constitute ignorance..."

The ploughman, the plough and the furrow are of one stuff.

Just as Emerson formulated the idea of unity in "Brahma", after having explained it roughly in prose in his essay on "Plato", so he formu-

[1] *Works*, VI, 426, n.

lated the idea of variety in his poem "Hamatreya", after having expressed the outline of it in the same prose. The idea underlying "Hamatreya" is that "the words *I* and *mine* constitute ignorance". This idea, in its full form, comes originally from a passage in the *Vishnu Purana*, which Emerson copied in his Journals for 1845, shortly before composing the poem. Thus "Hamatreya", unlike "Brahma", was inspired directly by a single passage from the Hindu. And as might be expected, it is less subtly expressed, and less perfectly formulated for this reason. Moreover, "Hamatreya" is dual in tone, in that it expresses both sides of the "Brahma" idea. It consists of a sort of argument between the Yankee and the Oriental Emerson. It describes the essentially Yankee feeling for variety, or property (for "the words *I* and *mine*"), and counters with the Hindu belief in unity ("the ploughman, the plough and the furrow are of one stuff"). Both the poem and the passage by which it was suggested are too long for complete quotation, but partial quotation from each will illustrate how Emerson's creative mind worked when reacting more immediately and less subtly to outside influence than it did in the case of "Brahma." Also the passages quoted may help to exemplify the development of the underlying idea.

"Hamatreya" begins with a striking expression of "difference" (from the Yankee point of view), works around to the statement of identity, expresses this in the "Earth Song" and closes with a rather trite moralistic quatrain:

Bulkeley, Hunt, Willard, Hosmer, Merriam, Flint,
Possessed the land which rendered to their toil
Hay, corn, roots, hemp, flax, apples, wool, and wood.
Each of these landlords walked amidst his farm
Saying, "'Tis mine, my children's, and my name's."

. . . .

Earth laughs in flowers, to see her boastful boys
Earth-proud, proud of the earth which is not theirs;
Who steer the plow, but cannot steer their feet
Clear of the grave.

. . . .

Ah! the hot owner sees not Death, who adds
Him to his land, a lump of mould the more.
Hear what the Earth says: —

"Mine and yours;
Mine, not yours.
Earth endures;
Stars abide —
Shine down in the old sea;
Old are the shores;
But where are the old men?"

. . . . . .

"They called me theirs,
Who so controlled me;

Yet every one
Wished to stay, and is gone,
How am I theirs
If they cannot hold me,
But I hold them?"

When I heard the Earth-song
I was no longer brave;
My avarice cooled
Like lust in the chill of the grave.

The above includes about half of "Hamatreya," and may be compared with the following short extract from the passage of the *Vishnu Purana* from which it developed.

These and other kings who ... have indulged the feeling that suggests "This earth is mine, — it is my son's — it belongs to my dynasty," —have all passed away... Earth laughs, as if smiling with autumnal flowers... I will repeat to you, Maitreya, the stanzas that were chanted by Earth...

How great is the folly of princes... "Thus," they say, "will we conquer the ocean encircled Earth;" and intent upon their project, behold not death, which is not far off... Foolishness has been the character of every king who has boasted, "All this earth is mine — everything is mine — it will be in my house forever," for he is dead.

These were the verses, Maitreya, which the earth recited and by listening to which ambition fades away like snow before the sun.[1]

Thus "Hamatreya" developed out of the

[1] *Journals*, VII, 127.

Hindu dialogue between Vishnu and Maitreya. The closeness of phrase and idea is obvious. The question remains only as to why Emerson changed the name in his title from "Maitreya" to "Hamatreya".

Both "Brahma" and "Hamatreya" show how Emerson worked over these foreign materials in his mind, and made poems from them. The striking thought of both is Hindu (the Yankee element in "Hamatreya" is introduced entirely for contrast). The two deal with different aspects of the same Hindu idea. "Hamatreya" expressed the feeling for the identity of matter under its various appearances in spite of the "magical illusions of reality" — the identity of earth and the human body. "Brahma" expressed the feeling for the identity of energy — of the human soul and the life-process. The two developed conceptions which were essentially Hindu. In them Emerson was reinterpreting his foreign material in American poems.

In "The Sphinx", however, the case is different. This poem is a much more original and complex one than the other two. It is possible that it was composed without thought of this Hindu idea. But it is interesting to study it with these others in mind, for it deals fundamentally with the same problem — that of the reappearance of the energy of the world under various disguises:

> Through a thousand voices
> Spoke the universal Dame,
> "Who telleth one of my meanings
> Is master of all I am."

And part of the stanza before this is very similar to a passage from the *Bhagavat Gîta*,[1] which reads as follows: "I am the light of the sun and moon.... fragrant smell in the earth, refulgence in fire: I am life in all beings." These similes also appear in "The Sphinx":

> She silvered in the moon
> She spired into yellow flame;
> She flowered in blossoms red;
> She flowed into a foaming wave;
> She stood Monadnoc's head.

Here it is only the phrase, "I am life in all beings" that does not seem to be echoed from the *Bhagavat Gîta*,[2] and that metaphor was to recur in "Brahma", later.

[1] "The Sphinx" was published in 1841 — two years before Emerson read the *Bhagavat Gîta*, but this passage may possibly have been in one of the "extracts" from it which he mentions reading earlier. It is from Chapter VII, verses 6–9.

[2] It would seem to strengthen the belief that "The Sphinx" was partly inspired by Oriental literature, that Thoreau, in recording his impressions of the poem in his Journals for 1841, illustrates and

It is interesting to follow this Hindu idea of "Brahma" and "Hamatreya", which Emerson had reincarnated in American literature, through the later writings of American poets; and in passing a relationship with Emerson's poems may be suggested for Whitman's "Pensive, on her dead gazing, I saw the Mother of All", for Mr. Sandburg's "Grass", and for "John Brown's Body". But a discussion of this relationship is outside the scope of this study.[1] As it is, the idea, especially of "Hamatreya", is closely related to Emerson's own later literary development.

This idea was not purely a poetic concept, but led to the prose of Emerson's essay on "Illusions", and engrossed him more and more in his later writings. Probably, indeed, "Illusions" owes as much to Hindu philosophy as any other single major idea of his. While "Brahma" was a development from his own "Over-Soul" idea, "Illusions" has less background in his earlier writing. Of course both ideas were prepared for by his reading of Plato and the Neoplatonists,

interprets many of its phrases and ideas with passages from *The Laws of Menu*, which he was then reading. (See *Thoreau's Journals*, I, 229.)

[1] Such a discussion will be found in *American Literature* (Nov. 1929), I, 233–242.

but his development of the doctrine of "Illusions" has an especially Oriental tinge.[1]

This doctrine occupied his mind especially in his latter years, and his essay entitled "Illusions" constitutes the logical completion and culmination of his thought. The very word, "illusions", appears frequently only in his mature vocabulary — after the beginning of the period of his Oriental reading. Yet, of course, the idea was not new to him, and in one passage of his essay, where he mentions "Yoganidra", one of the Hindu goddesses of Illusions, he also suggests a connection with his earlier thought. The Hindu belief that salvation was to be attained by seeing through "the magical illusions of reality", is much like Emerson's doctrine of "Nature as Discipline". So he writes:

> I find men victims of illusion in all parts of life. Children, youths, adults and old men, all are led by one bawble or another, Yoganidra,the goddess of illusion, Proteus, or Momus, or Gylfi's Mocking, — for the Power has many names, — is stronger than the Titans, stronger than Apollo. Few have overheard the gods or surprised their secret. Life is a succession of lessons which must be lived to be understood.

— Experience of the illusions of reality disci-

[1] For a contrary opinion see J. S. Harrison, *op. cit.*, pp. 266–272.

plines man to the understanding of the true meaning of life.

The idea of "Illusions" is not only comparable to Emerson's own earlier writing, it is (as has been noticed), related to the Platonic "variety", and to the "flowing" philosophy of the Greeks. Emerson traces this connection himself in his essay, and lest there should be any doubt as to which philosophy he considered most expressive of the idea, he specifically prefers the Hindus:

> The early Greek philosophers Heraclitus and Xenophanes measured their force on this problem of identity.... But the Hindoos, in their sacred writings, express the liveliest feeling, both of the essential identity and of that illusion which they conceive variety to be. "The notions, '*I am*', and '*This is mine*' which influence mankind, are but the delusions of the mother of the world. Dispel, O Lord of all creatures! the conceit of knowledge which proceeds from ignorance." And the beatitude of man they hold to lie in being freed from fascination.

In the next paragraph Emerson quotes a sentence of the Persians to the same purpose. So, even if the final paragraph of the essay, with its beautiful snow-storm simile, is comparable to passages from Plato and Plotinus, these passages have been so transformed as to be more Emersonian than Platonic, and the two Oriental quotations may be said to conclude the essay which Emerson, the American Scholar, was writing. It was Emerson, the Literary Artist, who concluded with similes suggested by Platonism.

One indication of how Emerson took his concept of Illusions from Hindu philosophy is the frequency with which he mentions Maia, the Hindu goddess of Illusion, in this connection. He once wrote a poem, or series of verses, entitled "Maia", beginning:

> *Illusion* works impenetrable
> Weaving webs innumerable...

And in two later essays, published after "Illusions" he continued his discussion of the idea. The first of these is "Works and Days", included in his *Society and Solitude* volume. Here he describes the illusions of the world at length, giving prominence to the Hindu interpretation, and mentioning Maia:

> Such are the days,... but what a force of *illusion* begins life with us and attends us to the end!... The Hindoos represent Maia, the illusory energy of Vishnu, as one of his principal attributes. As if... Nature employed certain illusions as her ties and straps, — a rattle, a doll, an apple, for a child; skates, a river, a boat, a horse, a gun, for the growing boy; and I will

not begin to name those of youth and adult, for they are numberless. Seldom and slowly the mask falls and the pupil is permitted to see that all is one stuff, cooked and painted under many counterfeit appearances...

This element of illusion lends all its force to hide the values of the present time...

It is the deep today that all men scorn... One of the illusions is that the present hour is not the critical, the decisive hour....

And again, in his next volume, Emerson describes the same idea in his essay on "Poetry and Imagination":

This belief that the higher use of the material world is to furnish us types or pictures to express the thoughts of the mind, is carried to its logical extreme by the Hindoos, who, following Buddha, have made it the central doctrine of their religion that what we call Nature, the external world, has no real existence, — is only phenomenal. Youth, age, property, condition, events, persons, — self even, — are successive *maias* (deceptions) through which Vishnu mocks and instructs the soul. I think Hindoo books the best gymnastics for the mind.

— As in his later essays, so in his later Journals, the Hindu doctrine of Illusions is often considered. The striking passage explaining the "science" of the Hindus has already been noticed, with its teaching that illusions should be set aside in order to regain union with the *paramâtman*, or Over-Soul. Just before making this significant entry, however, he had jotted down a series of notes which also brought together the ideas of "Maia" and "Brahma". And although these notes are apparently disconnected, they are mostly from the same source, and indicate the connection between the personified "Maya" — "that energy in numerous forms", and "Brahma", the impersonal, unified source of life.

> *Maya* (*Illusion*) *of the Hindoos*. Rudra says, "O thou, who, always unalterable, createst, conservest, and destroyest this universe, by the aid of Maya, that energy in numerous forms which... makes believe that it is distinct from thee, and gives to the world an apparent reality".—
> *Maya....*
> The Veda says: "The world is born of Maya."
> *Brahma qui n'a pas de qualités.*[1]

TRANSMIGRATION

The Hindu "Brahma" and "Maia", the Platonic "Unity" and "Variety", the Emersonian "Over-Soul" and "Illusions" — both ideas are fundamental to any abstract philosophy. They express necessary and elemental truths. They are two ideas which Emerson de-

[1] *Journals*, X, 159.

veloped, first from Platonism, and later from Hinduism, but which he surely would have developed somewhat for himself even without either of these philosophies. A third idea which he interpreted from the Hindu is more particularly Oriental, and so it is especially interesting to see his attempts to apply it to his own Yankee scheme of thought. This is the theory of metempsychosis, or the transmigration of souls.

In the Hindu system of thought, transmigration was the natural corollary of "Brahma" and "Maia". The vital force is the same in all beings; individual bodies give the illusion of reality, but actually are transient, dissolving at death; so it is natural that one unit of the vital force — one single soul — should be conceived as inhabiting different bodies in succession — as migrating from one to the other at death. This seemed to most Hindoos the natural conclusion of the simple idea of "Brahma". The highly spiritualized conception, described by Emerson, where "Brahma" is the inclusive, impersonal source of energy, into which all different units return at death and are merged and lost, was more advanced than the popular Hindu belief. This latter taught that, if the slayer think he slays, he is wrong, because the individual soul of the slain man will migrate at death into another individual body — be it man, or dog, or fish. And so Emerson wrote in his essay on "Immortality", connecting his idea historically with the doctrine of metempsychosis, — "for I know well that where this belief once existed it would necessarily take a base form for the savage and a pure form for the wise; — so that I only look on the counterfeit as a proof that the genuine faith had been there."

Emerson's most interesting description of this idea of transmigration occurs in his Journals, where he is using the idea for no particular purpose, but is only trying to clarify his own thoughts. Here, perhaps better than anywhere else, we can see his mind at its work of interpreting to itself the meaning of foreign ideas:

> *Metempsychosis.* For this Indian doctrine of transmigration, it seems easy of reception where the mind is not preoccupied... Here is a gentleman who abused his privileges when in the flesh as a gentleman, and curtailed therefore his amount of vital force. We cannot kill him, for souls will not die. This punishment, self-imposed, is, that he take such a form as his diminished vital force can maintain. Now it takes, to make a good dog, say, half a grain; to make a peacock, a quarter grain; to make a great general, a pennyweight; a philosopher, two; a poet, ten; and a good and wise man, a thousand pounds. Now our ill-

behaved man, on emerging from his rotten body, and a candidate for a new birth, has not capital enough to maintain himself as a man, and, with his diminished means, nothing is left for it but that he should take a turn through nature, this time as monkey. That costs very little, and by careful governance in the monkey form he shall have saved something and be ready at his return to begin the world again more decently say, as a dog. There he saves again, and, at the end of that period, may drop his tail, and come out Hottentot. Good Hottentot, he will rise, and one of these ages will be a Massachusetts man.

... Travelling the path of life through thousands of births.[1]

Shortly after this, the Journals again deal with the idea. This time Emerson mentions the theory of transmigration to explain how the Hindu widow can burn herself on her husband's funeral pyre. It is because she believes that her soul will be born again in a state similar to his, so that she may still accompany him, and guide him eventually to a higher state. And so "the flame of the funeral pile is cool to the widow". Then Emerson says significantly: "To this practical doctrine of Migration we have nothing corresponding. Ours is sentimental and literary." [2]

Indeed, except for the Journal passage first quoted Emerson never did try to interpret the

[1] *Journals*, VII, 93–4.

[2] *Ibid.*, VII, 120–1.

theory of transmigration practically. He saw that it was a superstition essentially Hindu. When he made use of it, he merely associated it with the ideas which, intellectually, were most like it. In this way he used it three times in his essay on "Swedenborg".

First he coupled it with the Platonic theory of Reminiscence, using both to explain the power of intuition possessed by certain men of religion:

> If one should ask the reason for this intuition, the solution would lead us into that property which Plato denoted as Reminiscence, and which is implied by the Bramins in the tenet of Transmigration. The soul having been often born, or, as the Hindoos say, "travelling the path of existence through thousands of births,"... there is nothing of which she has not gained the knowledge.

Here he is attempting to explain an intellectual phenomenon in terms of an old superstition. In a like manner he uses the theory again to explain the workings of Swedenborg's own mind, with its strange affinities and mysticisms:

> The metempsychosis which is familiar in the old mythology of the Greeks, collected in Ovid, and in the Indian Transmigration, and is there *objective*, or really takes place in bodies by alien will, — in Swedenborg's mind has a more philosophic character. It is subjective, or depends entirely upon the thought of the person.

Finally in summing up Swedenborg's qualities, he again likens him to a Hindu soul, seeking the unity of the law of right, in the variety of existence, saying:

> I think of him as of some transmigrating votary of Indian legend, who says "Though I be dog, or jackal, or pismire, in the last rudiments of nature, under what integument or ferocity, I cleave to right, as the sure ladder that leads up to man and to God."

In all of these cases Emerson used the theory of transmigration to explain intellectual phenomena. The common superstition enabled him to understand the peculiarities of thought of a powerful mind. He did not try to justify the superstition, he merely explained it by showing its relation to mental laws. But before making this interpretation for himself, he had already learned from the Platonists how such an interpretation of the law might be made. In his *Essays, First Series*, one of the two apparently Oriental references is to the theory of transmigration. He rationalizes this theory in an interesting way. But it appears that this rationalization is merely adapted from a Neoplatonic source quoted by his old book *The True Intellectual System*, by Cudworth. A comparison of the two passages reveals much of interest. In his "History" essay Emerson wrote:

> The transmigration of souls is no fable. I would it were; but men and women are only half human. Every animal of the barnyard, the field and the forest, of the earth and of the waters that are under the earth, has contrived to get a footing and to leave the print of its features and form in some one or other of these upright, heaven-facing speakers. Ah! brother, stop the ebb of thy soul,—ebbing downward into the forms into whose habits thou hast now for many years slid.

In Emerson's copy of Cudworth he had marked the passage:

> But as for that other transmigration of human souls into the bodies of brutes, though it cannot be denied but that many of the ancients admitted it also, yet Timaeus Locrus, and divers others of the Pythagoreans, rejected it, any otherwise than as it might be taken for an allegorical description of the beastly transformation that is made of men's souls by vice.[1]

Emerson's borrowing of this first interpretation from a Neoplatonic source argues many things. First, it adds to the conviction that by the time of publishing his *Essays, First Series*, Emerson had not begun to use his Oriental sources. Second, it shows that in this case, as

[1] *The True Intellectual System of the Universe*, I, 70. See also J. S. Harrison, *op. cit.*, p. 276.

in many others, he came to his Oriental reading fresh from Neoplatonic thought. The Neoplatonists introduced him to Oriental forms and ideas. Third, it illustrates the progress of Emerson's mind — first he adopted fully the Neoplatonic attitude toward transmigration, next (as in the "Swedenborg" essay) he attempted to relate the Hindu theory to general Platonic ideas; and later still (in his Journals) he tried to realize for himself the full import of the idea. But, unlike "Brahma", he never incorporated the transmigration idea into his own thought.

"FATE"

Yet these ideas have their parallels in modern scientific thought. It has been suggested that "Brahma" is merely a subtle, poetic expression of the law of conservation of energy. So even transmigration may foreshadow the modern theory of evolution. In a chance passage from his essay on "Fate", Emerson suggests the linking of these ideas. He illustrates his writings from the Hindu fables where

> Vishnu follows Maya through all her ascending changes, from insect and crawfish up to elephant; whatever form she took, he took the male form of that kind, until she became at last a woman and goddess,

and he a man and a god. The limitations refine as the soul purifies, but the ring of necessity is always perched at the top.

The quotation is not so important as the use Emerson makes of it. In the processes of transmigration or evolution described, the spiritual Vishnu must follow the material Maya, as the two work out their destiny in Nature. They are fated to accompany each other in the natural changes of things. It is what Emerson described earlier in the essay as "the despotism of race". Here he described the idea more clearly:

> It was a poetic attempt to lift this mountain of Fate, to reconcile this despotism of race with liberty, which led the Hindoos to say, "Fate is nothing but the deeds committed in a prior state of existence." I find the coincidence of the extremes of Eastern and Western speculation in the daring statement of Schelling, "There is in every man a certain feeling that he has been what he is from all eternity, and by no means became such in time." To say it less sublimely, — in the history of the individual is always an account of his condition, and he knows himself to be a party to his present estate.

The Hindu theory of "Fate" thus gave its color to Emerson's thought. The Hindus had said in effect: the deeds of earlier men whose souls have migrated into the bodies of men of a later generation have affected these later men, by increase or decrease of the vital force transmitted. Emerson interpreted: in the course of evolution, the deeds committed by men's ancestors have their effect on their descendants of a later generation. — It was the Biblical question: If the fathers have eaten sour grapes, shall the children's teeth be set on edge? The Hindus had answered in the affirmative — "Fate is nothing but the deeds committed in a prior state of existence." Emerson quoted their answer and their reasons, and developed his essay with these in mind, although he did not accept the answer to the full.

In one sentence of his essay on "Fate" he declares: "We cannot trifle with this reality, this cropping out in our planted gardens of the core of the world." More specifically, he had already noted in his earlier Journals: "In India, it [Fate] is the dread reality, it is the cropping out in our planted gardens of the core of the world: it is the abysmal Force, untameable and immense."[1] A close comparison of these statements is revealing. "Fate", as Emerson described it for himself, was significantly less than that Fate, which he found in Indian literature. For him it was "this reality", but not "this dread reality";

[1] *Journals*, VII, 123.

for him it was not "the absymal Force, untameable and immense", it was merely a force of Nature.

He had written at the beginning of his essay on "Fate": "The Hindu under the wheel is firm". At its conclusion he used a Hindu idea once again, but with a new note of joy which is not to be found in the Hindu originals: "Let us build altars to the Beautiful Necessity, which secures that all is made of one piece; that plaintiff and defendant, friend and enemy, animal and planet, food and eater are of one kind." In other words: let us realize that the Necessity is also Beautiful.

So Emerson used Hindu ideas as material for his essays and poems, but without accepting their conclusions. The Hindus had merely refined the materials of thought for him. "Trace these colossal conceptions of Buddhism and Vedantism home," he wrote, "and they are always the necessary or structural action of the human mind. Buddhism, read literally, the tenet of Fate..."[1] The ideas of "Brahma", of "Illusions", of Transmigration or Evolution, and of "Fate" are inevitable to any philosophy. The vital and distinguishing thing is the way in

[1] *Journals*, VII, 122.

which they are used, and the conclusions to which they lead.

Other ideas closely related to "Fate", Emerson found interestingly developed in Hindu literature. For instance, in his essay on "Worship", after elaborating the theory of "Fate" just described, he added a new Hindu definition of "Law":

> In the human mind, this tie of fate is made alive. This law is the basis of the human mind. In us, it is inspiration; out there in nature we see its fatal strength. We call it the moral sentiment.
>
> We owe to the Hindoo Scriptures a definition of Law, which compares well with any in our Western books. "Law it is, which is without name, or color, or hands, or feet; which is smallest of the least, and largest of the large; all, and knowing all things; which hears without ears, sees without eyes, moves without feet and seizes without hands."

In like manner Emerson had described the "Internal Check" in his Journals:

> *Vedanta. The Internal Check.* He who eternally restrains this and the other world, and all beings within; who, standing in the earth, is other than the earth; whom the earth knows not, whose body the earth is, who interiorly restrains the earth, the same is thy soul, and the Internal Check immortal.
>
> The internal check is the Supreme being.[1]

[1] *Journals*, VII, 110.

While earlier still he had found in his reading of the Vedas, "eternal necessity, eternal compensation".[1] — Fate, Law, Compensation — these were terms which often applied to the same idea. Emerson's essay on "Compensation" indeed, furnished him with much of the basis of thought for his later essay on "Fate". The change in title and point of view in the two is largely due to the progress of his Oriental reading.

BUDDHISM

The Hindu resignation to Fate — to the "dread reality, the abysmal Force" of the world, was something against which Emerson rebelled. Always motor-minded, he hated quietism. And as he associated quietism especially with Buddhism, he often criticized that religion. We have already noticed that he described Buddhism as "read literally, the tenet of Fate"; and, although he often confused it with the larger aspects of Hinduism, he seems to have formed certain definite ideas about it. In general, the confusion came first, and the definite reactions followed on his knowledge. For instance, he first called the *Bhagavat Gîta* "the much renowned book of Buddhism", and so

[1] *Letters of Emerson to a Friend*, p. 27.

showed his ignorance. But at this same time he was reading another book of some kind on "Buddhism",[1] which he often mentioned and quoted in his Journals. So he did gain an early knowledge of the religion, and was able to form fairly definite ideas of it.

First, Emerson felt the rational quality of it. His most repeated quotation is of "The Buddhist law of hospitality: 'Do not flatter your benefactors'";[2] which, he observes, is a "true law". Later, in his *Essays, Second Series*, he asserts significantly: "Nature will not be a Buddhist: she resents generalizing, and insults the philosopher at every moment." And still later, in his Journals for 1845, he connects "Buddha, or he who knows" with the "Icy light" of Plato, as follows:

> *Buddha, or he who knows.* Intellect puts an interval: if we converse with low things, — the interval saves us. But if we converse with high things, with heroic actions, with heroic persons, with virtues, the interval becomes a gulf, and we cannot enter into the highest good.
>
> *Icy light.* It is the chief deduction, almost the sole deduction from the merit of Plato....that his writings

[1] I have been unable to discover the actual title of this book. He probably read a book of Buddhism by Edward Upham later, but at this date he had not yet come upon it.

[2] *Journals*, V, 408; *Works*, I, 337; III, 163.

have not the vital authority which the screams of the prophets... the sermons of the unlettered Arabs and Jews possess.[1]

In these passages Emerson obviously considers Buddhism as a rational philosophy rather than as a religion — and probably he was fundamentally right in doing so. For it is the intellectual element of Buddhism that sets it off from the emotionalized idealism of Hinduism. For Emerson, Buddha was the knower, and not the seer.

But for Emerson, Buddha was a special kind of philosopher. He wrote: "The Buddhist ... is a Transcendentalist",[2] and illustrated his assertion by citing: "his conviction that every good deed can by no possibility escape its reward." In his essay on "Poetry and Imagination" he quotes Buddha again, as illustrating the transcendentalist doctrine of "Nature as Language", as we have noticed: "This belief that the higher use of the material world is to furnish us types or pictures to express the thoughts of the mind, is carried to its logical extreme by the Hindoos, who, following Buddha, have made it the central doctrine of their religion..." Later on in the same essay, he remarks: "We see railroads, mills,

[1] *Journals*, VII, 110–11. [2] *Works*, I, 337.

and banks, and we pity the poverty of these dreaming Buddhists. There was as much creative force then as now, but it made globes and astronomic heavens, instead of broadcloth and wine-glasses".

Perhaps the chief thing that distinguishes Buddhism from the rest of Hindu thought in Emerson's writing is that Buddhism is the one Indian doctrine to which he ever expressed a decided aversion. The basis of this aversion lay somewhat in the over-rational quality which he felt to underlie it, and somewhat in its Fatalism. But also, I believe, he was repelled by the concept of Nirvana. In his Journals, he wrote:

> This remorseless Buddhism lies all around, threatening with death and night... Every thought, every enterprise, every sentiment, has its ruin in this horrid Infinite which circles us and awaits our dropping into it. If killing all the Buddhists would do the least good, we would have a slaughter of the Innocent directly.[1]

And again, more sweepingly:

> *Buddhism.* Winter, Night, Sleep, are all the invasions of eternal Buddh, and it gains a point every day. Let be, *laissez-faire*, so popular now in philosophy and in politics, that is bald Buddhism; and then very

[1] *Journals*, VI, 318.

fine names it has got to cover up its chaos withal, namely, trances, raptures, abandonment, ecstasy, — all Buddh, naked Buddh.[1]

These two passages of disparagement are the only ones of the sort. It is notable that they were written early in the course of Emerson's acquaintance with the Hindu literature — in 1842–3. Buddhism was the first type of Hinduism to which he reacted in his Journals, and part of his distrust of it, may be due to its unfamiliarity. The isolated concept of Nirvana has from the first been intimately connected with Buddhism by Western scholars; and that, combined with a lack of the emotional element in Buddhist thought, is probably enough to account for Emerson's aversion to it.

IDENTITIES AND DIFFERENCES

Having paid his homage, as for the human race, to the Illimitable, he then stood erect, and for the human race affirmed, 'And yet things are knowable!' — that is, the Asia in his mind was first heartily honored,... and now, refreshed... the instinct, of Europe, namely, culture, returns; and he cries, 'Yet things are knowable!'... There is a scale.

— Thus Emerson had written of Plato, and thus it might well be written of Emerson. His mind

[1] *Journals*, VI, 382.

was never more than half Oriental, and even when he wrote "Brahma", he organized it into a most perfectly balanced and proportioned poem, in conventional, Western metre. In "Hamatreya" he had expressed the feeling of Difference as well as that of Identity, and thus produced a poem dual in mood and idea.

Enthusiasts sometimes speak as though Emerson's ideas were all Eastern, even as if they were all expressed in the Hindu Scriptures. Mr. Charles Malloy, to whom Emerson lent his copy of the *Bhagavat Gîta*, said that "on reading the book he found in it the whole of Emerson's philosophy."[1] And discussions such as this paper attempts are liable to draw the circle of influence too widely and inclusively.

For instance parallels could be, and have been drawn between Emerson's doctrine of Self-Reliance, and the teaching of the Hindus. In his essay on "Aristocracy" he quotes from the *Laws of Menu* concerning a lesson "which every day returns to mind, 'All that depends on another gives pain; all that depends on himself gives pleasure; in these few words is the definition of pleasure and pain.'" And in the *Bhagavat Gîta* occurs a passage more strikingly

[1] D. L. Maulsby, *Emerson*, p. 123.

Emersonian in its final advice, perhaps, than any other of its sort in literature:

> The Lord is seated in the region of the heart of all beings.... With him seek shelter in every way; by his favor you will obtain the highest tranquillity, the eternal seat. Thus have I declared to you the knowledge more mysterious than any mystery. Ponder over it thoroughly *and then act as you like.*[1]

— But Emerson had fully developed his doctrine of Self-Reliance before beginning to read the *Bhagavat Gîta.*

Again, we have already remarked on the attitude toward Law which Emerson found attractive in the Hindoo. Yet he also liked the feeling for action and freedom which he found there, and in his essay on "Swedenborg" he writes: "That is active duty", say the Hindoos, "which is not for our bondage; that is knowledge, which is for our liberation: all other duty is good only unto weariness."

Finally, there are three doctrines sometimes connected with these Indian sources, which, I believe, Emerson derived from the Neoplatonic writings rather than from the Hindu. The first of these he quoted from the Hindus in his essay on Goethe saying: "Children only, and not

[1] Chapter XVIII, 65. The italics are added.

the learned, speak of the speculative and practical faculties as two. They are but one, for both obtain the selfsame end..." In his earlier essay, "The Poet", which is full of Neoplatonic material, he had written "Words and deeds are quite indifferent modes of the divine energy. Words are also actions, and actions a kind of words."

Second, Emerson's theory of "nature, as a symbol or manifestation of the deity", [1] clearly was not derived from the Hindu, although parallels may be found; for Emerson's first book, *Nature*, was published in 1836, before his Hindu reading began, and to it was attached a motto from Plotinus.

Third, Emerson noted in his Journal for 1845: "As for 'shunning evils as sins,' I prefer the ethics of the *Vishnu*: see beyond." [2] Here again is a parallel between the two on the doctrine that evil is mere negation. But Emerson had expressed this doctrine in his Divinity School Address in 1838, and the actual source of his concept is again probably Plotinus. — Thus, although many of Emerson's specific ideas found reinforcement in the Hindu Scriptures, most of

[1] D. L. Maulsby, *Emerson*, p. 127, maintains the opposite opinion.

[2] VII, 124.

them had been originally derived or created from other sources.

There are many ideas, even, which Emerson found in the Hindu Scriptures which did not reinforce his theories at all. Their belief in a "deaf, unimplorable fate", which he fastened on as the central doctrine of their philosophy, he used, but did not share. We have seen that he disliked the quietism of the Buddhists, especially associating it with "Winter, night, sleep." Finally, there were traits in the Hindu religion which had influenced him against it from the first. These can be summed up under what the *Edinburgh Review* had called "its quantity and its absurdity" on the one hand — that is, its formalism, its detailed ceremonial, its ritual; and on the other hand "its cruelty and its sensuality" — that is, its fundamental belief in the inferiority of woman, its primitive sexual morality, and its unrestraint. The qualities which made *Mother India* a best seller in 1928 were emphasized by the writers and reviewers of 1818. Emerson was fully cognizant of them when he wrote in 1840: "Nothing is easier than to separate what must have been the primeval inspiration from the endless ceremonial nonsense which caricatures and contradicts it through every chapter." [1]

[1] *Letters of Emerson to a Friend*, p. 27.

HINDU ESSAYS ON EMERSON

If Emerson did not accept the whole of Hindu literature, he did value the essential spirit of it. He read it constantly in his later years, and embodied many of its teachings in his latter essays and poems. He wrote of its Fatalism, and he described its theory of Illusion. He interpreted its fundamental belief in the unity at the heart of nature. He imbued himself more deeply with its thought than did any other great author of his day. He felt his own spiritual affinity for the Hindus. "If I trust myself in the woods or in a boat upon the pond," he wrote, "nature makes a Bramin of me presently." [1]

We have already seen that Emerson never went all the way in his Orientalism, however. He qualified his extravagant admiration for Hindu thought with a New England shrewdness. He never trusted himself to become wholly a Brahmin.

With this in mind, it is interesting to learn the attitude of Hindu students to Emerson. Two essays have been written by East Indians in appreciation of him: one by Protap Chunder Mozoomdar shortly after Emerson's death, and one by Herambachandra Maitra, in 1911, almost

[1] *Letters to a Friend*, p. 27.

thirty years later. These embody two different points of view, and seem to be typical. The first is more enthusiastic and unreserved, the second more considered and critical. The two balance each other, and show that Emerson has been accepted by India much as he accepted it — with enthusiasm, but also with respect for differences of time and race.

Mozoomdar, as we have seen, wrote that "Emerson had all the wisdom and spirituality of the Brahmins." His praise is chiefly of this spirituality, marking Emerson off from other Western writers; but sometimes his praise goes farther:

> Amidst this ceaseless, sleepless din and clash of Western materialism, this heat of restless energy, the character of Emerson shines upon India serene as the evening star. He seems to some of us to have been a geographical mistake. He ought to have been born in India. Perhaps Hindoos were closer kinsmen to him than his own nation, because every typical Hindoo is a child of Nature.[1]

If this ascription of Hindu relationship is extreme, it should be remembered that it was written as a sort of personal memorial and tribute from India:

[1] *The Genius and Character of Emerson*, 367. The essay is entitled "Emerson as Seen from India".

Long, long had we heard of his name and reputation. We wondered what manner of man he was. When at last I landed on your continent, how glad I should have been to sit at his feet and unfold before him the tale of our woe and degradation! But he has gone to his rest...[1]

Herambachandra Maitra, on the other hand, has written a more scholarly article, recognizing the qualities which differentiate Emerson from the Brahmins of India, and mark him as a native of the New World. With Emerson he at first couples Wordsworth, as also expressing spiritual truths like those of Hindu literature:

Hence the power with which Wordsworth and Emerson appeal to the Oriental mind. They translate into the language of modern culture what was uttered by the sages of ancient India in the loftiest strains. They breathe a new life into our old faith, and they assure its stability and progress by incorporating with it precious truths revealed or brought into prominence by the wider intellectual and ethical outlook of the modern spirit.[2]

But Emerson, of course, was the writer who actually had read what the sages of ancient India taught. And so it was of him that Maitra concludes:

[1] *The Genius and Character of Emerson*, p. 371.

[2] *Harvard Theological Review*, IV, 403. The essay is entitled "Emerson from an Indian Point of View."

In India the influence of Emerson has been deeply felt by many of those who have received Western education. It would be well if his influence extended to larger numbers. But the loftier the aims of the teacher, the smaller the band of disciples; and many, it must be admitted, are repelled by the peculiarities of Emerson's style.... Amidst the perplexities created by the conflict of the past and the present, of the East and the West, he is a safe guide; and amidst the depressing influences of life he is an unfailing source of strength and inspiration.[1]

Since Emerson was not wholly a Brahmin, it is only natural that his writings should not be accepted unreservedly by the Hindus. That his writing does appeal to them greatly, these two writers testify. Other studies have been made of him by other Hindus, but these are not immediately available. It is enough that Emerson's love of Hindu philosophy helped him to a wider and richer development of his own thought, and that it gave this thought a more universal appeal than that of other Western thinkers. His work represents, as Maitra writes, "the harmonious union of the modern spirit with the noblest teachings of ancient times".

[1] *Harvard Theological Review*, IV, 417.

LIST OF HINDU AUTHORS OR BOOKS QUOTED OR READ BY EMERSON

(When possible, the translation which Emerson used has been specified. The date given is that of first mention by Emerson. The number indicates frequency of mention, in years. In general these titles are taken from the annual reading lists in the *Journals*, and from the Notes to the Centenary Edition of Emerson's *Works*, with additions and corrections.)

The Mahabharata, (1830, 3)
  a) *apud* Gérando, (a very brief description).
  b) *apud* W. R. Alger, *Poetry of the East*, (selections).
  c) *Nala and Damayanti*.
The Vedas, (1839, 6)
  a) Various sources.
  b) *Rig Veda Sanhita*, (read late in life).
Vyasa, or Viasa, (1834, 4)
  (This fabulous "compiler" was credited both with the Mahabharata, and the Vedas, and the title may refer to either of these.)
Calidasa, or Kalidasa, (1837, 4)
  a) *Megha Duta*, *apud Asiatic Journal*.
  b) *Sakoontala* or *The Lost Ring*.
Vishnu Purana, (1845, 7)
  probably tr. by H. H. Wilson, (London,1840).
Bhagavat Geeta (1845, 5)
  tr. by Sir Charles Wilkins, (1785).
Code of Menu, or Institutes of Menu, (1836, 6)
  probably tr. by Sir William Jones, (London, 1825).
"Buddha", (1838, 2)
  unidentified.
Vishnu Sarna, (1841, 3).

Upanishad, (1856, 3)
tr. by E. Roer, *Biblioteca Indica*, vol. XV, (Calcutta, 1853); contains the "Katha Upanishad", among others.

H. T. Colebrooke, *Essays on the Vedas*, etc. (1845, 1)

"Hindu Mythology and Mathematics", *Edinburgh Review*, vol. XXIX.

"To Narayena", (1822, 2)
tr. by Sir William Jones.

CHAPTER VI

PERSIAN POETRY

Wine that is shed
Like the torrents of the sun
Up the horizon walls.

THE Persian poets probably affected Emerson more profoundly than any other Oriental writers except the Hindus — and, of course, the Neoplatonists. He came upon them later in life than he did upon Hindu Literature, but was attracted to them more immediately. He first read selections from them in 1841; in 1842 he wrote his poem "Saadi" for *The Dial*, and in 1843 he read the *Gulistan*,[1] and confided to his Journals that "In Saadi's *Gulistan* I find many traits which comport with the portrait I drew [in the poem "Saadi"]."[2] In 1846-7 he read all the Persian poets more fully in the German anthology of Von Hammer Purgstall, and to some extent, perhaps, in Chodzko's *Specimens of Ancient Persian Poetry*.[3] Throughout the rest of

[1] In the notes to Emerson's poem "Saadi" (IX, 447), the date is erroneously given as 1848. It is correctly given as 1843 in a note to his essay on Persian Poetry (VIII, 414).

[2] *Journals*, VI, 463.

[3] See *Journals*, VII, 280.

his life he continued to read them — usually in selections, although in 1853 the *Shah Nameh* of Firdousi is listed among his reading. And he noted down many comments on these poets in his Journals, and quoted them often in his Essays.

Most striking of all, however, is the fact that Emerson wrote two essays and two poems dealing with Persian poetry. First of these in importance is the essay of that title, included in *Letters and Social Aims*. Second is his poem "Saadi," first published in *The Dial*. Third is the Preface which he supplied to the first American edition of Saadi's *Gulistan*, in translation, published in 1865 by Ticknor and Fields. And last is a group of "Fragments on the Poet and the Poetic Gift", which is an interpretation of Hafiz and Saadi, a good deal idealized. To these may be added a few poems of Persian influence now published in the *Uncollected Writings*. All these are original essays and poems by Emerson. But he also made many translations of Persian poems from Von Hammer Purgstall, some of which are now published in the Centenary Edition.[1] If to this is added the fact that the Centenary Edition contains very full notes to his essay on "Persian Poetry", culled from his Journals and

[1] IX, 298–305.

Letters, it will be seen how abundant is the material on this subject.

And yet more remains to be said than is apparent. In the first place Emerson never attempted to characterize Hafiz very fully, nor to contrast Hafiz and Saadi as individuals. His remarks on Persian poetry are usually general. And so a comparison of what he considered the individual characteristics of Saadi and of Hafiz may prove illuminating. In the second place, two of Emerson's best, and apparently most original poems were partially inspired by his reading of Persian poetry; namely, "Bacchus" and "Days". This fact is not generally recognized, and may be developed further. Last, and most interesting of all, however, is the strange fact that Emerson never expressed what was probably the chief reason for his love of Persian poetry. After a complete reading of his comments on and quotations from the Persian, this becomes apparent; and at least one explanation may be suggested for the omission. Since this throws much light on his attitude towards Hafiz and Saadi as his ideal poets, the general characteristics which he found in the Persians may be summarized from this new point of view.

The most important question may be considered first. In his essay on "Persian Poetry", Emerson speaks of the "complete intellectual emancipation" which Hafiz communicates to the reader. Probably he never came nearer than this to stating explicitly his reason for taking Hafiz and Saadi as his ideal poets. In the Journals he had written of Hafiz in the same tone: "He is not scared by a name, or a religion. He fears nothing. He sees too far; he sees throughout; such is the only man I wish to see and to be. The scholar's courage is as distinct as the soldier's or statesman's and the man who has it not cannot write for me." [1]

But this intellectual liberty which for Emerson was the chief characteristic of Hafiz and the other Persian poets, arose largely from their new attitude towards life, and fate; and this, in turn, arose from their reaction against the relentless fatalism of the Mohammedan religion.[2] Yet Emerson, whenever he deals with the Persian writers as a class, invariably calls them fatalists.

In the essay on "Persian Poetry", itself, he wrote:

[1] *Journals*, VII, 328.

[2] Many of the later Persian poets were influenced by the doctrines of Sufi mysticism. Philosophically, the reaction of the Persian poets from fatalism may be explained by reference to these doctrines. The present discussion attempts only to point out the obvious divergence, without tracing the causes of it.

> Religion and poetry are all their civilization. The religion teaches an inexorable destiny. It distinguishes only two days in each man's history, — his birthday, called *the Day of the Lot*, and the Day of Judgment. Courage and absolute submission to what is appointed him are his virtues.

And he took the same tone in the Preface which he wrote for Saadi's *Gulistan*, in 1865. He dealt with Hafiz and Saadi:

> In common with his countrymen, Saadi gives prominence to fatalism, — a doctrine which, in Persia, in Arabia, and in India, has had in all ages a dreadful charm. "To all men", says the Koran, "is their day of death appointed, and they cannot postpone or advance it one hour."

Here Emerson couples the Koran and the Persian poets, even though on the next page he writes of Saadi that "He celebrates the omnipotence of a virtuous soul."

Lastly, a quotation from the beginning of Emerson's essay on "Fate" may suggest a reason for his repeated statement: "The Turk, the Arab, the Persian, accepts the foreordained fate:

> On two days it steads not to run from thy grave,
> The appointed and the unappointed day;
> On the first, neither balm nor physician can save,
> Nor thee, on the second, the Universe slay."

This quatrain expresses the fatalism of Mohammed, and, if it had been written by one of the "Persian poets", would fully justify the charge of fatalism made by Emerson against all the Persians. It proves, indeed, to be a quatrain which Emerson did translate from Von Hammer Purgstall's *Anthology of Persian Poetry*. But actually it was written by one "Ali ben Abu Taleb", who is none other than the Caliph Ali of early Mohammedanism. Thus it naturally expresses the fatalism of the Koran, of the 7th century, and cannot be classed with the Persian poetry of the 10th to the 15th centuries. Von Hammer's inclusion of it with other later Persian poetry naturally misled Emerson, and explains, in part, at least, why Emerson repeatedly describes all the Persian poets as fatalists.

Actually, however, the Persian poets were very often poor Mohammedans. Most of them lived six or more centuries after Caliph Ali and Mohammed. They had become freed from too abject a surrender to fate. Emerson in reality liked them because they expressed the joy and lightness that came from this new emancipation, although he still called them fatalists in writing of them.

That this is true is shown by the many Persian quotations, mostly from Hafiz, that Emerson used in his essays on "Fate", "Power", and

"Illusions". In "Fate" he speaks approvingly of "sallies of freedom. One of these is the verse of the Persian Hafiz, ''Tis written on the gate of Heaven, "Woe to him who suffers himself to be betrayed by Fate!"''"[1] And again, in the same essay, Emerson writes: "We learn that the soul of Fate is the soul of us, as Hafiz sings,

> Alas! till now I had not known,
> My guide and fortune's guide are one."

In his essay on "Power", Emerson again writes of: "This affirmative force... 'On the neck of the young man', said Hafiz, 'sparkles no gem so gracious as enterprise.'" And finally, on the very last page of his book, at the end of the essay on "Illusions", Emerson wrote: "It would be hard to put more mental and moral philosophy than the Persians have thrown into a sentence,

> Fooled thou must be, though wisest of the wise:
> Then be the fool of virtue, not of vice."

It would be hard to find a more striking group of quotations than the above, to refute the charge of fatalism brought against the Persian poets, and Emerson has given these quotations prominent place in his last great book of essays.

[1] VI, 29. See also *Journals*, VII, 269.

But more of the same sort are to be found cited from Hafiz in his essay on "Persian Poetry". He quotes Hafiz,

> I batter the wheel of heaven
> When it rolls not rightly by;
> I am not one of the snivellers
> Who fall thereon and die.

And again:

> Loose the knots of the heart; never think on thy fate:
> No Euclid has yet disentangled that snarl.

Or we may see the explanation of some of the recklessness of Hafiz in the following: "'On every side is an ambush laid by the robber-troops of circumstance; hence it is that the horseman of life urges on his courser at headlong speed.'"

So it was that the Persians, with Hafiz at their head, escaped from the absolute fatalism of their religion by living at the maximum — as well as they knew how. It was this quality of fulness and joy that Emerson most liked in them, but it was also this that sometimes resulted in the reckless abandon of hedonism, as in Hafiz's verses:

> Drink, hear my counsel, my son, that the world fret thee not.
> Though the heart bleed, let thy lips laugh, like the wine cup;
> Is thy soul hurt, yet dance with the viol strings...

But as Emerson wrote, "it is the spirit in which the song is written that imports," and to Hafiz wine was the symbol of this new escape from Fate — the symbol of Life. So Emerson took it in his own poem "Bacchus", as "the remembering wine". And so he translated Hafiz approvingly in his Journals.[1]

Come let us strew roses,
And pour wine in the cup
Break up the roof of heaven
And throw it into new forms
. . . . . .
So will I, with the cupbearer
Shatter the building of woe.

Thus, as Emerson wrote, "Hafiz praises wine, maidens, boys, birds, mornings, and music, to give vent to his immense hilarity and sympathy with every form of beauty and joy."[2] And on the next page he compares Hafiz and Shakspeare, saying: "A saint might lend an ear to the riotous fun of Falstaff; for it is not created to excite the animal appetites, but to vent the joy of the supernal intelligence."

Hafiz was one who vented this supreme joy. And yet even more than Hafiz Emerson takes Saadi as the type of "joygiver and enjoyer". In his essay on "Shakspeare; or, the Poet", he

[1] VII, 181. [2] *Works*, VIII, 249–50.

writes that "One more royal trait properly belongs to the poet. I mean his cheerfulness, without which no man can be a poet, — for beauty is his aim.... Beauty, the spirit of joy and hilarity, he sheds over the universe.... Homer lies in the sunshine; Chaucer is glad and erect; and Saadi says, 'It was rumored abroad that I was penitent, but what have I to do with repentance?'" — Here Emerson uses the same language in speaking of Shakspeare and Hafiz; of Homer and Saadi, and joins them all together, because both Shakspeare and Hafiz expressed for him "hilarity", and "joy", and gave emancipation, and both Homer and Saadi "lay in the sun". Indeed, a large part of the poem on "Saadi" is the interpretation of the Persian as the poet of joy. He is "the cheerer of men's hearts"; the "son of eastern morning". He is the antagonist of the sad-eyed Fakirs who "swiftly say Endless dirges to decay."

And to the same intent Emerson remarked in his essay on "Swedenborg", that "this man, who, by his perception of symbols, saw the poetic construction of things... remained entirely devoid of the whole apparatus of poetic expression, which that perception creates." And, mentioning Saadi, Emerson seems to hint that Swedenborg failed to be a poet, because he lacked all feeling for the joy of the world.

Thus, Emerson loved both Hafiz and Saadi because they were joyful. And they were joyful because, trusting in themselves and in the fulness of life, they had escaped from the ambush of fatalism. They had at least partially freed themselves from Mohammedanism. But this does not mean that they were irreligious, although they seemed so at times, just as Emerson seemed to his contemporaries. Indeed, Hafiz wrote:

> I am: what I am
> My dust will be again.[1]

And Emerson also quoted him in his essay on "Worship":

> At the last day men shall wear
> On their heads the dust.

Usually, however, it is the use of the religion of the Persian poets to teach the meanness of the world, and so to give them the power to escape from it, as when Hafiz writes: "Our father Adam sold Paradise for two kernels of wheat; then blame me not if I hold it dear at one grapestone."

However, the Persian poets found the con-

[1] *Works*, VIII, 250.

structive and positive side of religion in their love of beauty. Emerson tells of how Saadi came on a man reading the Koran aloud in a harsh voice, and asked him why he was reading. "He replied, 'I read for the sake of God.' The other rejoined, 'For God's sake, do not read; for if you read the Koran in this manner you will destroy the splendor of Islamism.'"[1] And that Saadi felt that he himself was writing his own poetry for the sake of God is shown by the whimsical legend of one who saw "angels descending with salvers of glory in their hands. On asking one of them for whom those were intended, he answered, 'For Shaikh Saadi of Shiraz who has written a stanza of poetry that has met with the approbation of God Almighty.'"[2]

And so likewise Hafiz replied to the vizier returning from Mecca: "Boast not rashly, prince of pilgrims, of thy fortune. Thou hast indeed seen the temple; but I, the Lord of the temple. Nor has any man inhaled from the musk-bladder of the merchant or from the musky morning wind that sweet air which I am permitted to breathe every hour of the day."[3]

[1] *Works*, VIII, 121.
[2] *Journals*, VI, 465.
[3] *Works*, VIII, 254.

So Hafiz, having seen beauty, had seen the Lord of the temple; and Saadi had written a poem so beautiful that it had pleased even God Almighty. Yet these poets expressed no unbridled worship of beauty — rather they felt an independent love of it. Perhaps the finest line of Hafiz is one which describes just the qualities that beauty lacks, for, as he writes,

Neither endurance nor truth belongs to the laugh of the rose.[1]

What gave both Hafiz and Saadi the courage to free themselves from Fate, and to express the joy of life; to leave the Koran and to devote themselves to the expression of pure beauty, and yet to save themselves from an absolute hedonism, is something which is hardly ever explicit in their poetry, and yet is always there. In the Emersonian phrase it is simply the virtue of Self-Reliance. Trusting to it the Persians could dare to "batter the wheel of heaven, when it rolled not rightly by". This virtue takes many forms in their writing, but never is expressed merely for its own sake. Rather it gives to Saadi the assurance of pleasing God with his poetry; it keeps Hafiz from being one of the "snivellers", who falls on the wheel of fate; and it gives to the

[1] *Works*, VIII, 256.

joy of both the solid foundation of a consciousness of the value of life.

Even Emerson did not dwell much in detail on their quality of Self-Reliance. But one passage near the beginning of the poem "Saadi" stands out:

> Saadi loved the race of men, —
> No churl, immured in cave or den;
> . . . . . .
> But he has no companion;
> Come ten, or come a million,
> Good Saadi dwells alone.

And it is suggestive that this passage is also used as the motto of Emerson's essay on "Clubs".

It is another aspect of this Self-Reliance that Emerson ascribed to Hafiz in "Persian Poetry", saying; "That hardihood and self-equality of every sound nature, which result from the feeling that the spirit in him is entire and as good as the world, which entitle the poet to speak with authority... are in Hafiz, and abundantly fortify and ennoble his tone." And Hafiz himself had written:

> To the unsound, no heavenly knowledge comes.[1]

To the self-reliant and healthy man, mere self-expression may become a virtue. With this

[1] *Journals*, VIII, 459.

in mind, an entry in Emerson's Journals is more easily understood. The following outburst occurs after the reading of Hafiz: "Expression is all we want: not knowledge, but vent: we know enough; but have not leaves and lungs enough for a healthy perspiration and growth. Hafiz has!... 'Keep the body open,' is the hygeian precept.... Large utterance!" [1] And in like manner Emerson wrote of Saadi, saying: "He has also that splendour of expression which alone, without wealth of thought, sometimes constitutes a poet, and forces us to ponder the problem of style." [2]

This splendor of expression Emerson would perhaps have explained in part as resulting from the sincere utterance of a man who is true to himself — from perfect self-expression. But in the poem "Saadi", Emerson explains this "large utterance", also, as resulting from the poet's use of nature as language, thus connecting it with an old doctrine of his. Of Saadi, he wrote:

> In his every syllable
> Lurketh Nature veritable.
>
> . . . .
>
> Suns rise and set in Saadi's speech.

---

[1] *Journals*, VII, 279.

[2] "Preface" to Saadi's *Gulistan*, p. ix.

And also in the "Fragments on the Poet" Emerson describes how

> Those idle catches told the laws
> Holding Nature to her cause.
>
> . . . .
>
> God only knew how Saadi dined;
> Roses he ate, and drank the wind.
>
> . . . .
>
> He felt the flame, the fanning wings,
> Nor offered words till they were things.
>
> . . . .
>
> Sun and moon must fall amain
> Like sower's seeds into his brain,
> There quickened to be born again.

Emerson believed that for the ideal poet, and also for Saadi, Nature is language, and the splendid expression is the most natural one. And for him, high and low Nature are the same.

In both poems dealing with Saadi, Emerson developed this doctrine of the democracy, or self-equality of Nature. It helped him, as he also felt it had helped the Persian poets, to justify an absolute self-reliance to a common man. Because, if all Nature is divine, absolute beauty is to be found in all common-place objects, and a common man may become a perfect poet by understanding Nature perfectly. And the joy of complete self-expression is possible to all men.

Indeed, the poem "Saadi" teaches this doctrine of the value even of low Nature as its chief lesson, and its final section might be quoted entire, but a few lines will be enough:

Eat thou the bread which men refuse.

. . . .

Nor mount, nor dive; all good things keep
The midway of the eternal deep.

. . . .

On thine orchard's edge belong
All the brags of plume and song.

. . . .

Toil whistles as he drives his cart.

In "Fragments on the Poet", the same is to be found:

Said Saadi, "When I stood before
Hassan, the camel-driver's door,
I scorned the fame of Timour brave.
. . . . I
Worship Toil's wisdom that abides."

And the same doctrine struck Emerson when he first read Hafiz, for his first Journal entry concerning him is the following: "Hafiz defies you to show him or put him in a condition inopportune or ignoble. Take all you will, and leave him but a corner of Nature, a lane, a den, a cowshed... he promises to win to that scorned spot, the light of the moon and stars, the love of men, the smile of beauty, and the homage of art."[1] And later in his Journals he exclaimed of Hafiz: "Sunshine from cucumbers! Here was a man who has occupied himself in a nobler chemistry of extracting honor from scamps, temperance from sots, energy from beggars, justice from thieves, benevolence from misers. He knew there was sunshine under those moping, churlish brows, and he persevered until he drew it forth."[2]

It is this joyful humanity and love of all Nature that attracted Emerson to Hafiz and Saadi. They, too, had set up for themselves a new set of values, based on joy in life — and not on the materialism of the world, nor on the fatalism of a single religion. They, too, were happy. They had seen Nature and had found her beautiful, and had expressed their joy in her beauty:

> And ever the spell of beauty came
> And turned the drowsy world to flame.[3]

Hence Emerson took them as his ideal poets. For, as he translated Hafiz,

> ... in the world of love
> And estimation true
> The heaped up harvest of the moon
> Is worth one barley-corn at most,
> The Pleiads' sheaf but two.

---

[1] *Journals*, V, 562. [2] *Ibid.*, VII, 182.

[3] IX, 321. "Fragments on the Poet".

The Persians transported him into the "world of love, And estimation true", where beauty was a stronger force than even thought, and joy could free itself from fatalism. Perhaps one quatrain of Hafiz which Emerson translated, expresses this beauty and freedom more perfectly and purely than any other poem of his, and the quotation of it may fittingly close a consideration of the Persians as Emerson's ideals in poetry. The imagery is curiously suggestive of the English mystic, Blake, yet it was Hafiz who wrote:

> See how the roses burn!
> Bring wine to quench the fire!
> Alas! the flames come up with us,
> We perish with desire.

We have seen how, to Hafiz and Saadi as ideal poets, Emerson ascribed freedom of thought and freedom of spirit, which resulted in their feeling of absolute joy in the world; how they showed him a sincerity and self-reliance, which assured them of the basic value of life; and finally how they possessed for him a perception of beauty in Nature and in Man, which inspired their poetic expression. All these qualities Emerson possessed in himself, insofar as, according to his own standard, he was a true poet. But there are other qualities which he found in the Persians which were not so fundamentally those of an ideal poet, but which he nevertheless held in common with them. These may be mentioned in passing.

The first is the inspirational quality of woman. This Emerson connected with the Persians only once, but in a very striking passage, in his Second Series of Essays, asking:

> Was it Hafiz or Firdousi that said of his Persian Lilla, She was an elemental force, and astonished me by her amount of life, when I saw her day after day radiating, every instant, redundant joy and grace on all around her? She was a solvent powerful to reconcile all heterogeneous persons into one society: like air or water, an element of such great range of affinities that it combines readily with a thousand substances. Where she is present all others will be more than they are wont.... She did not study the Persian grammar, nor the books of the seven poets, but all the poems of the seven seemed to be written upon her. For though the bias of her nature was not to thought, but to sympathy, yet was she so perfect in her own nature as to meet intellectual persons by the fulness of her heart, warming them by her sentiments.[1]

This passage is especially significant in that it again combines Emerson's appreciation of the feminine force of the world, with his interest in

[1] III, 151–2.

the Orient, whose genius he also felt to be feminine.

Second, and more abstract, is the appreciation of Love and Friendship common to Emerson and to the Persians. Several of the "Translations" included in Emerson's Poems, are from Persian poems dealing with Love, of which the "Flute" from Hilali may be mentioned as perhaps the best; and many more deal with Friendship. The anonymous Persian proverb "Either death or a friend" is quoted in "Social Aims". Once again Ali is quoted among the Persian poets, when his verses on friendship are translated in the *Poems*.[1] In "Considerations by the Way", also, Hafiz and Ali are cited together, Hafiz as writing "Thou learnest no secret until thou knowest friendship." This saying is repeated in "Persian Poetry". And in the Journals Emerson translated Hafiz roughly:

> Give high the prized stone
> Only to sacred friends alone.[2]

Finally, it is notable that the Persians, with almost all other Oriental nations, expressed the law of Compensation. The best saying to this effect is probably that of Hafiz: "Here is the sum, that, when one door opens, another shuts."[3]

[1] IX, 302. [2] *Journals*, VIII, 487. [3] *Works*, VIII, 245.

But also the equivalence of the poetry and joy of Hafiz to the riches and power of the Shah is often declared, as

> I have no hoarded treasure,
> Yet have I rich content;
> The first from Allah to the Shah
> The last to Hafiz went.[1]

These, then, are some of the coincidences of thought and temper between Emerson and the Persians. Emerson admired Hafiz and Saadi greatly, and took them as his ideals in poetry. But Emerson never gave absolutely unqualified praise to any writer, and these two were no exception. The faults he noticed in them are interesting.

Of these, the most obvious is the Persians' extreme of license, and their hedonism. One would expect that Emerson might have been repelled by these; yet actually their lack of sober morality offended him less than any other of their faults, and he excused it more readily. For, as we have seen, "it is the spirit in which the song is written that imports."

As has already been suggested, Emerson often implied the coupling of Hafiz and Saadi with

[1] *Works*, VIII, 253. See also VIII, 254; and *Uncollected Writings*, p. 189.

Shakspeare: and took each in turn as his ideal poet, using much the same terms of praise and blame for each. Thus, in "Persian Poetry", he had written that "A saint might lend an ear to the riotous fun of Falstaff", in order to explain the high poetic license of Hafiz. And towards the end of his essay on Shakspeare, he had quoted Saadi approvingly. In his *Poems* also, there occur the following interesting lines:

> "A new commandment", said my smiling Muse,
> "I give my darling son, Thou shalt not preach;"
> Luther, Fox, Behmen, Swedenborg, grew pale,
> And, on the instant, rosier clouds upbore
> Hafiz and Shakspeare with their shining choirs.[1]

Of course this argues high praise on Emerson's part for Hafiz. But it also suggests the chief criticism which is implicit in all the minor faults which he could find in Persian poetry. This is the criticism which he expresses concerning Shakspeare, in *Representative Men*; that Shakspeare rested in the mere beauty of the natural world. "He was the master of the revels of mankind.... — Are the agents of nature, and the power to understand them, worth no more than a street serenade? One remembers again the trumpet text of the Koran, — 'The heavens and the earth and all that is between them, think ye

[1] *Works*, IX, 297.

that we have created them in jest?'" Here the criticism of Shakspeare is equally applicable to the Persian Poets, and the text from the Koran is further suggestive of the justice of this application.

Indeed, towards the end of his life, Emerson clearly voiced this criticism in his Journals, as when in 1866 he declared: "Hafiz can only show a playing with magnitudes, but without ulterior aim." [1] And later in the same year he repeated and enlarged this:

> Hafiz's poetry is marked by nothing more than his habit of playing with all magnitudes, mocking at them. What is the moon, or the sun's course or heaven, and the angels, to his darling's mole or eyebrow?... I do not know but the sad realist has an equal or better content in keeping his hard nut.... I will not be the fool of fancy, nor a child with toys. The positive degree is manly, and suits me better: the truth is stranger and grander than the gayest fable.[2]

And so, although Emerson made due allowance for the hedonism of the Persians, and enjoyed them none the less for it, he disliked their constant extravagance of tone, of subject, of imagery. He noted: "'Tis with difficulty that we wont ourselves in the language of the Eastern poets, and their melodramatic life. When we go

[1] *Journals*, X, 144. [2] *Ibid.*, X, 167.

down to the Long Wharf we do not find an ivory boat and a pink sea."[1] In the same way he wrote apologetically in his Preface to the *Gulistan*: "I do not know but, at the first encounter, many readers take an impression of tawdry rhetoric, an exaggeration, and a taste for scarlet, running to the borders of the negrofine." But "these blemishes disappear or diminish on better acquaintance."

In this same Preface he apologizes at some length for most of the faults of the Persian poets — for their license, their absurd flattery of the Shah, for their extreme inconsecutiveness of thought, for their poverty of poetic imagery.

Nevertheless, Emerson enjoyed and was immensely influenced by his reading of them, and sometimes he even loved their faults. So he confided to his Journals: "I suppose, every one has favorite topics, which make a sort of museum or privileged closet of whimsies in his mind, and which he thinks is a kind of aristocracy to know about. Thus, I like to know about lions, diamonds, wine, and Beauty; and Martial and Hafiz."[2] And he never renounced this love, for Hafiz and Saadi are among the last poets that in his Journals he mentions reading.

[1] *Works*, VIII, 421. [2] *Journals*, VIII, 488.

"DAYS" AND "BACCHUS"

Two of Emerson's best poems were inspired in part, at least, by his reading of Persian poetry. Of these, "Days" is less clearly imbued with its spirit, and yet certainly contains Persian and Oriental elements. The poem is short, and may be quoted entire:

> Daughters of Time, the hypocritic Days,
> Muffled and dumb, like barefoot dervishes,
> And marching single in an endless file,
> Bring diadems and fagots in their hands.
> To each they offer gifts after his will,
> Bread, kingdoms, stars, and sky that holds them all.
> I, in my pleached garden, watched the pomp,
> Forgot my morning wishes, hastily
> Took a few herbs and apples, and the Day
> Turned and departed silent. I, too late,
> Under her solemn fillet saw the scorn.

In the Journals for May 24, 1847, the first entry is the following: "The days come and go like muffled and veiled figures sent from a distant friendly party, but they say nothing, and if we do not use the gifts they bring, they carry them as silently away." In a note Mr. Edward Emerson has observed that this sentence was later embodied in the poem "Days". And then comes this interesting statement: "In his latter years, he said that, while he held it as perhaps his best, he could not recall the writing of it."

In other words, this poem was probably formed more or less unconsciously out of the elements in Emerson's mind at about this time. Other entries in the Journals of this date are suggestive. The second Journal passage for May 24, 1847, is the translation of a long poem of Hafiz. In this occurs the following familiar motif:

> Surely I have no treasure,
> Yet am I richly satisfied;
> God has given that to the Shah,
> And this to the beggar.

This may suggest, even if vaguely, the line from "Days":

> To each they offer gifts after his will.

And it may be further noted that Emerson felt that the Oriental temperament possessed a special genius for gifts.[1]

The next line of the poem "Days" suggests a trick of Hafiz which Emerson himself remarked upon — namely, a "playing with magnitudes":

> Bread, kingdoms, stars, and sky that holds them all.

And lastly, the second line of "Days" is most clearly Persian, for "barefoot dervishes" formed

[1] See note to the essay "Gifts", III, 165, and 327.

a staple of the imagery of the Persian poets, and appear in many of Emerson's translations from them.[1] Mention of this simile in "Days" gives a clear indication of the trend of Emerson's mind at this time.

Thus, the general idea of the poem — that God offers gifts "to each after his will" is largely Oriental. Emerson was translating Hafiz at the time that the idea of the poem occurred to him. And finally, the simile of the Dervishes is purely Persian. It is true that the imagery of "Days" also grew from his experience of an old New England village custom, that neighbors on New Year's Eve should bring baskets of gifts secretly and leave them on their friends' door-steps, and depart. But the high poetic quality of the poem, its moral and basic idea, are Oriental, and may be connected with Emerson's reading of the Persians.

The case of "Bacchus" is more definite. Since we have Emerson's own statement of it, a detailed comparison between the lines of the poem, and the probable sources of inspiration for them, may for the most part be omitted.[2]

[1] See Index of the *Works*, under "Dervishes".

[2] For a statement of the other side of this question — that "Bacchus" had its chief source in Proclus and the Neoplatonists, see John S. Harrison, *The Teachers of Emerson*, p. 275.

The poem was written in 1846, at the same time that Emerson was beginning his reading of Hafiz. In July of the year he wrote to Miss Elizabeth Hoar concerning several poems which he was composing, and which he was impatient to show her, "especially some verses called 'Bacchus' — not, however, translated from Hafiz."[1] If, in a letter to a literary friend, he thought it necessary to specify that "Bacchus" was not a translation from Hafiz, the implication is obvious that the poem was practically inspired by his reading of the Persian.

The tone of freedom and exaltation in "Bacchus" is that of Hafiz. Three lines of the poem are perhaps as fine as any that Emerson ever wrote, and at the same time express the spirit of Persian poetry at its best. They describe the

> Wine that is shed
> Like the torrents of the sun
> Up the horizon walls.

They connect Hafiz's wine of freedom with his sunshine of joy. And they also recall Emerson's comment on Hafiz, that: "He knew there was sunshine under those churlish brows... Now... the sunshine is out and all flowing abroad over the world."[2]

[1] *Works*, IX, 443. [2] *Journals*, VII, 182.

HAFIZ AND SAADI, INDIVIDUALS

Among the Persian poets Emerson appreciated the lyric greatness of Hafiz, and would probably have acknowledged his supremacy; but he felt himself personally attracted more to Saadi, and concentrated his interest on the lesser poet, especially in the earlier years of his acquaintance with the Persians. Hafiz's name occurs 14 times in his annual reading-lists, and Saadi's 12. But Saadi is among the very last authors mentioned in the Journals, being listed in the year 1872. Thus it appears that Emerson's interest in these two Persians was nearly equal. Beyond them he only comments on Firdousi, "the Persian Homer", once or twice, and does not single out any of the others. Apparently Omar Khayyam never especially attracted him.

It has been suggested that Goethe first directed him to Hafiz and Saadi.[1] This seems probable, inasmuch as Emerson had been learning German in order to read Goethe not many years before this, and so would have been especially apt to know of Von Hammer's German translation, and to interest himself in it.

Goethe mentioned Hafiz with particular

[1] See note to *Works*, IX, 500.

praise. But Emerson appeared at first rather indifferent to him. In 1846 he noted in the Journal: "Hafiz, whom I at first thought a cross of Anacreon and Horace, I find now to have the best blood of Pindar in his veins. Also of Burns."[1] The authors with whom Emerson compared his favorites are always interesting, and here we see Hafiz first as a poet merely of love and wine, but later as one of the really great lyrists of the world. And as already noticed, Emerson coupled Hafiz and Shakspeare several times in his later writing.

Emerson felt that Hafiz had a greater poetic power and intensity than Saadi, but he also felt an occasional hardness and bitterness in him. This feeling, however, he seldom fully expressed. A quatrain of Hafiz which Emerson translated probably shows Hafiz's spirit at its best, and yet suggests what Emerson did not approve in him:

> Bethink, poor heart, what bitter kind of jest
> Mad destiny this tender stripling played;
> For a warm breast of maiden to his breast,
> She laid a slab of marble on his head.[2]

In contrast to this, Emerson always dwelt on the broad humanity and benevolent wisdom of

[1] *Journals*, VII, 170. [2] *Works*, IX, 300.

Saadi. He felt a more friendly worldliness in him. Again, the names with which Emerson couples him are suggestive: "Æsop, Saadi, Cervantes", he wrote, "know the realities of human life." And with greater praise: "Through his Persian dialect he speaks to all nations, and, like Homer, Shakspeare, Cervantes, and Montaigne, is perpetually modern."[1] Still again, in the Journals, he wrote: "Like Montaigne, he learns manners from the unmannerly." And "there is the spice of Gibbon in him."[2]

The mere fact that Saadi lived to be more than a hundred years old, and wrote much of his work in his latter years, suggests this quality of mellow wisdom which Emerson loved in him. In the essay on "Books", Emerson mentions Saadi twice, and passes over Hafiz. First he includes the *Gulistan* in a "class of books which may be called Table Talks". And later he repeats the title among "such books as have acquired a semi-canonical authority in the world, as expressing the highest sentiment and hope of nations."

In this short summary, Emerson's poem "Saadi" has not been discussed in detail, as also the remarks dealing with Hafiz in "Persian Poetry", and the verses dealing with each in

[1] "Preface" to the *Gulistan*, p. viii. [2] *Journals*, VI, 463.

"Fragments on the Poet". It may be mentioned, however, that Saadi appears much oftener as the ideal poet in Emerson's writings than does Hafiz. Probably a reason for this is that Emerson felt himself much more nearly akin to him. Most of the qualities which he ascribes to the Persian might be used to describe Emerson's own writing. And so a descriptive paragraph from his Preface to Saadi's *Gulistan* (not reprinted elsewhere), may be used to characterize both Saadi and Emerson. If the name "Emerson" were substituted for "Saadi", the description would probably be even more accurate and true than as it appears on Emerson's page; — for Saadi, it must be remembered, is often only the ideal which Emerson set up for himself:

Saadi, though he has not the lyric flights of Hafiz, has wit, practical sense, and just moral sentiments. He has the instinct to teach, and from every occurrence must draw the moral, like Franklin. He is the poet of friendship, love, self-devotion, and serenity. There is a uniform force on his page, and, conspicuously, a tone of cheerfulness, which has almost made his name a synonyme for this grace. The word *Saadi* means *fortunate*. In him the trait is no result of levity, much less of convivial habit, but first of a happy nature, to which victory is habitual, easily shedding mishaps, with sensibility to pleasure, and with resources against pain. But it also results from the habitual perception of the beneficent laws that control the world. He inspires in the reader a good hope. What a contrast between the cynical tone of Byron and the benevolent wisdom of Saadi![1]

Hafiz was more akin to Byron.

LIST OF PERSIAN POETS QUOTED OR READ BY EMERSON

(The number indicates frequency of mention, in years.)

Hafiz (14), Saadi (12), Firdousi (4), Enweri (3), Ammar Asjedi of Merw (2); Ferradeddin, Jelaleddin, Nisami, Jami, Ali ben Abu Taleb (the Arabian), Omar Khayyam, Ibn Jemin, Feisi, Kermani, Hilali, Seyd Nimetollah of Kuhistan (once each).

LIST OF BOOKS CONCERNING PERSIAN POETRY READ BY EMERSON

Von Hammer Purgstall:
  a) Various German translations from the Persian.
  b) *Geschichte der Schönen Redekunste Persiens.*

Firdousi, The *Shah Nameh.*
Saadi, The *Gulistan.*
A. Chodzko, *Specimens of Ancient Persian Poetry.*

[1] pp. vii–viii.

CHAPTER VII

ARABIAN LITERATURE AND THE KORAN

The true romance which the world exists to realize will be the transformation of genius into practical power.

— EMERSON'S *Works*, III, 86.

PERSIAN poetry was so beautiful that it often seemed to monopolize Emerson's literary interest, and keep him from reading other related Oriental literatures. It attracted him so that he wrote of it repeatedly in his prose and in his verse. Yet important as it was, and beautiful as it is in itself, it has dazzled readers into overlooking other phases of his Orientalism; and especially is this true of Arabian literature, and of the Mohammedan writings in particular. Emerson gave much attention to them, and it is only the lack of a focus of interest that kept him from writing of them more fully. As it is, he quoted them constantly and at length, to illustrate all phases of his thought, and he suggested several original ideas in connection with them which are striking.

Arabian literature was in many ways complementary to Persian. Emerson had written of the Persians that: "Religion and poetry are all their civilization" [1]; while in another passage he had declared that "Religion and poetry are all the civilization of the Arab." [2] Both statements are true, but Emerson might have said more particularly that religion comprised all the civilization of the Arab, and poetry all that of the Persian. For, although the Persian poets were Mohammedans, they were not deeply so; and although Arabian literature was poetic, it was so only incidentally. The true Arabian poets had not been translated in Emerson's time. Of course the two literatures coincide at times, and Emerson actually confused them, taking several early Arabian quotations from Von Hammer Purgstall's translations of the *Persian Poetry*; but for the most part they are distinct.

The Arabian genius was essentially for religion, but for a religion closely allied to beauty. Immediately after asserting that religion and poetry constituted all Arabian civilization, Emerson illustrated with a quotation from the Koran. "The ground of Paradise", said Mohammed, "is extensive, and the plants of it are hallelujahs." Here he had found the two ele-

[1] *Works*, VIII, 238. [1] *Ibid.*, X, 177.

ments combined in a poetic religion; but more often Mohammedan literature showed a duality of tone and spirit. Emerson continues: "Religion and poetry: the religion teaches an inexorable destiny; it distinguishes only two days in each man's history, the day of his lot, and the day of judgment. The religion runs into asceticism and fate.[1] " And he goes on to show that the poetry is revealed especially in the material civilization of the Arab — in his diamonds and pearls, in his spices and costly silks and gorgeous dyes.

This duality between the poetry of material objects and the religion of the spirit recurred constantly in the Arabian literature which Emerson read. Spirit and flesh, religion and poetry appeared side by side, and often conflicted. All the books from which he drew fall into one or the other class.

First, of course, he read the *Arabian Nights* — in 1822, and in later years. Here the material was that of poetry and of imaginative fiction. But at this same time he was reading Gibbon's *Decline and Fall of the Roman Empire*, of which Chapters 50 to 52 chronicle the rise and fall of the Saracen Empire, with various quotations

[1] *Works*, X, 177.

from the Koran, and many details from history. Then he read the *Oriental Geography* of Ibn Haukal, from which he drew at least one anecdote of a fabulous sort. There followed in 1834 a book of *Arabian Proverbs*, from which he excerpted at various times.[1] In 1837 he lists the *Historia Muslemica* of Abulfeda, and in 1840, Ockley's *History of the Saracens*; both of which gave him valuable information concerning Mohammedanism, and the Koran. In 1841 he was reading Carlyle's essay on Mohammed in *Heroes and Hero Worship*. In 1843 he records in his Journals an enlightening conversation with a certain Mr. Vethake in New York on the subject of Mohammed. And in 1845 he was reading a strange and interesting book with the philosophic side of later Mohammedanism, called *Akhlak-y-Jalaly*, which he cites in his essay on Plato. This was a translation of a 15th century Persian text which purported to give the "Practical Philosophy of the Mohammedan People, exhibited in its professed connection with the European, so as to render either an introduction to the other... The most successful efforts of the entire people to reconcile the Greek philosophy with the social and religious system of the Moham-

[1] See *Journals*, III, 260 and 331.

medans may be said to be concentrated in this work".[1] Here, then, he became acquainted with the philosophy of Mohammedanism, with additions.

Apparently Emerson did not read the Koran save in short extracts till 1855, or perhaps later, when the book is often listed. As usual his earlier knowledge had come through indirect citations; although the knowledge was none the less real. Later, in 1862, he drew many striking sayings from a modern book: *Les Chevaux de Sahara*, by a captive Arabian emir, Abd-el-Kader. And finally, the next year several Arabian quotations occur in Emerson's Journal from the Persian translation of Von Hammer Purgstall.

Thus the first and last books dealing with Arabia which Emerson read were secular books of proverbs, of imaginative fiction, and of poetry. In the central, productive period of his life, influencing him more powerfully perhaps, were the books of religion, philosophy, and history. Considered as a whole, these books of Arabian literature were read by Emerson throughout his life, were quoted in his earliest as well as in his latest writing, and furnished many striking confirmations of his thought.

[1] See note to *Works*, IV, 312.

The quality of all this literature which most attracted him was its raciness — in the literal sense. It sprang from the soil, and was the natural expression of this race of desert people. It had the ring of reality in it. Of the secular literature, the *Arabian Nights* were pure folk tales, and the collections of Proverbs were popular; while the religious utterances of Mohammedanism were true to the temper of the people to which they belonged. Emerson had written: "It is almost the sole deduction from the merit of Plato that his writings have not... the vital authority which the screams of prophets and the sermons of unlettered Arabs and Jews possess.[1]" Arabian literature, both secular and religious, had this vital authority preëminently. Curiously enough, the figure of Mohammed did not seem to overshadow Arabian literature as that of Confucious did overshadow Chinese. Mohammed was the mouthpiece of Arabia.

Although the religious aspect of Arabian literature bulked largest to Emerson, the poetic and fanciful aspect of it first attracted him. This was most like what he had found in the Persian poets, and the Arabian differed from the Persian chiefly in its more popular origin. The *Arabian*

[1] *Works*, IV, 76.

Nights, for instance, expressed for him the same spirit of joy and light-hearted fancy which he had found in the Persians. In his essay on "Perpetual Forces", he made of Scheherazade the universal type of the joy of youth:

> Would you know where to find her? Listen for the laughter, follow the cheerful hum, see where is the rapt attention, and a pretty crowd all bright with one electricity; there in the center of fellowship and joy is Scheherazade again.

And in "Eloquence", he speaks of "the Arabian Nights. Scheherazade tells these stories to save her life, and the delight of young Europe and young America in them proves that she fairly earned it." Or, as he later exclaimed: "The Arabian Nights' Entertainment... — what mines of thought and emotion, what a wardrobe to dress the whole world withal, are in this encyclopedia of young thinking".[1] And yet he felt that "The more indolent and imaginative complexion of the Eastern nations makes them much more impressive by these appeals to the fancy.[2]

Again among other secular books, Emerson found the Arabian proverbs to his liking, perhaps even more than their more literary fiction.

[1] *Works*, VII, 106. [2] *Ibid.*, VII, 71.

One of his favorite sayings, which he twice quotes in his Essays, emphasizes also the healthy enjoyment of life: "'Allah does not count from life the days spent in the chase', that is, those are thrown in".[1] And he adds: "A man must be able to escape from his cares and fears, as well as from hunger and want of sleep; so that another Arabian proverb has its coarse truth: 'When the belly is full, it says to the head, Sing, Fellow!'" The way to religious truth led through the frankness of simplicity and proverbial life. Emerson never scorned the racy or the popular — rather he sought it out. He adopted another Arabian proverb to explain his own habits: "The barber learns his art on the orphan's face' — that is, "When a village Lyceum Committee asks me to give a lecture, and I tell them I will read one I am just writing, they are pleased. I 'try it on' them; 'The barber learns his trade on the orphan's chin!'"[2]

Sometimes these Arabian sayings took the form of highly poetic similes or exaggerations. Thus Emerson was impressed with the sentence: "He fled on a mare that would catch a falling tear"; and also copied into his Journals another passage from *Les Chevaux de Sahara*: "These are

[1] *Works*, VIII, 280, and V, 70.

[2] *Journals*, III, 26.

not courses for your horses... you Christians, who go from Algiers to Blidah, thirteen leagues, as far as from my nose to my ear, and yet believe you have made something of a journey."[1]

Two stories of Arabian hospitality which he copied had the same fabulous and poetic appeal. The first came from Von Hammer's translation: "'Bring in the guest', said Hatem Tai; 'I never eat alone'.—Hatem Tai, who roasted his wonderful horse to entertain the messengers of the Sultan who had come to ask the horse in the name of the Sultan".[2] In the same vein, in his earlier essay on "Heroism", Emerson wrote that "Ibn Haukal, the Arabian geographer, describes a heroic extreme in the hospitality of Sogd, in Bukharia. 'When I was in Sogd I saw a great building, like a palace the gates of which were open and fixed back to the wall with large nails. I asked the reason, and was told that the house had not been shut, night or day, for a hundred years...!'"

This heroic extreme occurs in much Arabian literature, and relates it to the Persian. In a long passage Emerson tells the Arabian story of Kurroglou, which Longfellow has versified in "The Leap of Roushan Beg", heading it "*Orien-*

[1] *Journals*, IX, 408. [2] *Ibid.*, IX, 539.

tal Superlative. The life of the Arabian a perpetual superlative." For an example of this, we may take the address of Kurroglou to his horse, and the story of his leap:

"On! on! my Soul, Kyrat, carry me to Chamley Bill. Alas! my horse, let me not look upon thy shame. I will have thee wrapped in velvet trappings. I will shoe thy fore and hind legs with pure gold. O my Kyrat, my chosen one of five hundred horses... thou shalt have a bath in a river of red wine."

Kurroglou...continued to walk Kyrat until the foam appeared in his nostrils. At last he selected a spot where he had room enough for starting, and then, giving his horse the whip, pushed him forward. The brave Kyrat stood on the very brink of the precipice; the whole of his four legs were gathered together like the leaves of a rosebud; he struggled a while, then gave a spring, and leaped to the other side of the ravine, nay he cleared two yards farther than was necessary. As for Kurroglou, even his cap did not move on his head...[1]

The difference between the poetic and the heroic superlative is slight. Extreme heroism and courage are the characteristic virtues of the Arab, both as expressed in history and in imaginative literature. So to the essay on "Heroism", in which he had spoken of "the heroic extreme of hospitality in Bukharia", Emerson prefixed a striking motto from Mohammed: "Paradise is

[1] *Journals*, VII, 281–2.

under the shadow of swords." And in the verses immediately following, he wrote:

> The hero is not fed on sweets,
> Daily his own heart he eats.

Similarly, Emerson copied in his Journals another quotation from the Koran, that "The saint's best blush in Heaven is from his heart-blood's red." [1]

Emerson exemplified this virtue of heroism by other Arabian illustrations. In his essay on "Courage", he asserted:

> Each [hero] respects the other. If opportunity allowed, they would prefer each other's society, and desert their former companions. Enemies would become affectionate. Hector and Achilles, Richard and Saladin, General Daumas and Abd-el-Kader, become aware that they are nearer and more alike than any other two, and, if their nation and circumstance did not keep them apart, would run into each other's arms.[2]

And the efficacy of heroism in social progress he described in another essay:

> The vigor of Clovis the Frank, and Alfred the Saxon, and Alaric the Goth, and Mahomet, Ali and Omar the Arabians, Saladin the Kurd, and Othman the Turk, sufficed to build what you call society on the spot and in the instant when the sound mind in the sound body appeared.[3]

[1] *Journals*, X, 134. [2] *Works*, VII, 271. [3] *Ibid.*, I, 317.

Heroism includes many of the Arabian teachings — for instance that of Self-Reliance. In his essay of that title, Emerson made use of a striking sentence ascribed to the Caliph Ali: "'Thy lot or portion of life', said the Caliph Ali, 'is seeking after thee; therefore be at rest from seeking after it.'" Ali, the hero, knew the virtue of self-reliance. Emerson also quoted Abd-el-Kader to the same intent, in his essay on "Behavior": "'Take a thornbush', said Abd-el-Kader, 'and sprinkle it for a whole year with rose-water; — it will yield nothing but thorns. Take a date-tree, leave it without water, without culture, and it will always produce dates. Nobility is the date-tree, and the Arab populace is the bush of thorns.'" Still again, Emerson quoted the Koran that "A mountain may change its place, but a man will not change his disposition." [1]

Emerson had written that a man must take himself for better or for worse as his portion. The Arabian believed that the hero achieves his greatness by an absolute reliance on his own temperament. It is striking that Emerson's belief also corresponded with Mohammed's, that an excess of humor was incompatible with this

[1] *Works,* VII, 64.

high sincerity. The hero must be absolutely single-minded, and must not stoop to ridicule. The religious seriousness of the Koran is often reflected in Emerson's writings, and perhaps the most striking passage from it which he used is to this effect. It occurs in his essay on "Shakspeare", and seems to reënforce his own most intense mood. He writes: "One remembers again the trumpet-text in the Koran, — 'the heavens and the earth and all that is between them, think ye we have created them in jest?'" In a later essay Emerson also quoted Mohammed:

> True wit never made us laugh. Mahomet seems to have borrowed by anticipation of several centuries a leaf from the mind of Swedenborg, when he wrote in the Koran:
>
> "On the day of resurrection those who have indulged in ridicule will be called to the door of Paradise, and have it shut in their faces when they reach it. Again, on their turning back, they will be called to another door, and again, on reaching it, will see it closed against them; and so on, *ad infinitum*, without end."[1]

In the Journals Emerson noted that the Caliph Ali "possessed a vein of poignant humor, which led the Soliman Farsy to say of a jest he

[1] *Works*, VIII, 98.

one day indulged in, This it is which has kept you back to the fourth (Abu Beker, Omar, and Othman, having been successively elected before him.)" [1]

It is significant that this Caliph Ali, although one of the great figures of Islam, is more typical of Persian Mohammedanism, than of Arabian. It is his story that Matthew Arnold has told in his essay on "A Persian Passion Play"; and it is he whom Emerson found quoted among the Persian poets in Von Hammer's translations. His nature did not possess the absolute single-mindedness typical of Mohammedanism — it was more thoughtful and complex. So Emerson quoted Mohammed as saying in praise of him: "Various are the Virtues, O Ali, by which men are brought near to their Creator, but thou by thy intellect art created near, and standest before them by many degrees of approach." [2] In his essay on "Aristocracy", Emerson had also noted that "In his consciousness of deserving success, the caliph Ali constantly neglected the ordinary means of attaining it." It is certain that Mohammed's followers did not share their prophet's trust, and Ali's couplet which Emerson quoted in *The Conduct of Life*, was inspired

[1] *Journals*, VII, 109. [2] *Works*, X, 525.

by his experience. "An Eastern poet, Ali Ben Abu Taleb, writes with sad truth:

He who has a thousand friends has not a friend to spare,
And he who has one enemy shall meet him everywhere."[1]

Absolute seriousness and absolute sincerity was demanded by Mohammedanism. Emerson quoted Mohammed in his essay on "Worship": "'There are two things', said Mahomet, 'which I abhor, the learned in his infidelities, and the fool in his devotions.'"[2] If Mohammed often appears to Westerners not to have been absolutely sincere, a further text of Emerson's may be cited: "'God has granted', says the Koran, 'to every people a prophet in its own tongue.'"[3] Mohammed certainly was sincere and serious in his belief that he was a divinely inspired prophet, and this belief formed the foundation of Islam.

Mohammed's intense seriousness was typical. It is this which has made Mohammedanism seem fanatical to all other nations. At the beginning of his essay on "Plato", Emerson noted: "Among secular books, Plato only is entitled to Omar's fanatical compliment to the Koran, when he said, 'Burn the libraries; for their value

[1] *Works*, VI, 273.
[2] *Ibid.*, VI, 240. See also *Journals*, VII, 107.
[3] *Ibid.*, IV, 225.

is in this book.'" The prime requisite of a Mohammedan was a fanatical and heroic belief. Emerson copied the Koran that "Hell is a circle about the unbelieving."[1] Those who were capable of the most absolute belief in God, and in Mohammed as the prophet of God, were the best Mohammedans.

Most important of all, this Mohammedan belief was not a vague and empty thing. It led to practical results. It united the dual nature of the Arabian — joining his sensual worldliness with his spiritual religion. It spanned the gap between flesh and the spirit. For instance, Occidentals have often remarked on the sensuousness of the Mohammedan paradise — "whose breadth equalleth the Heavens and the earth."[2] This paradise was essentially for the warriors of Islam — for the men who should put their belief into practice. In his essay on "Immortality" Emerson noted that "Mahomet in the same mind declared, 'Not dead, but living, ye are to account those who are slain in the way of God.'" Emerson also quoted the Caliph Ali: "'If knowledge', said Ali the Caliph, 'calleth unto practice, well; if not, it goeth away.'"[3] With most Mohammedans, knowledge of Islam called to battle for Islam.

[1] *Journals*, X, 134. [2] *Ibid.* [3] *Works*, I, 222.

The direct appeal of Mohammedanism was inspiring to the Arab. In his life no complex civilization intervened between his faith and his practice of it. His religion was all his civilization. In "Man the Reformer" Emerson described the rise of the Saracen religion as due to the impelling power of its ideal:

> Every great and commanding moment in the annals of the world is the triumph of some enthusiasm. The victories of the Arabs after Mahomet, who, in a few years, from a small and mean beginning, established a larger empire than that of Rome, is an example. They did they knew not what. The naked Derar, horsed on an idea, was found an overmatch for a troop of Roman cavalry... The women fought like men, and conquered the Roman men. They were miserably equipped, miserably fed. They were temperance troops. There was neither brandy nor flesh needed to feed them. They conquered Asia, and Africa, and Spain, on barley...

In the days of Mohammed, this religion had inspired an heroic practice. Recently this religious heroism has been again proved, and it is interesting to see how well Emerson's observations concerning Arabia still hold. He wrote: "Civilization is a re-agent, and eats away old traits. The Arabs of today are the Arabs of Pharoah, although the Briton of today is a very different person from the Briton of Cassibelaunus and Ossian."[1] So T. E. Lawrence, the latest prophet of Arabia, has proved; and his description of the Arabian nature is scarcely less remarkable than his actual feat of leading his army of Arabs, in the Great War, to their final triumph. His own eloquence and idealism served to inspire a new "Revolt in the Desert", and he writes:

> Arabs could be swung on an idea as on a cord... Without a creed they could be taken to the four corners of the world (but not to heaven) by being shown the riches of the earth and the pleasures of it; but if on the road, led in this fashion, they met the prophet of an idea, who had nowhere to lay his head and who depended for his food on charity or birds, then they would all leave their wealth for his inspiration. They were incorrigibly the children of the idea, feckless and color-blind, to whom body and spirit were forever and inevitably opposed.[2]

The dual nature of the Arab could, and still can, be unified and made effective by an ideal inspiration. For a time Mohammed and his followers had been able to unite bodily and spiritual powers, and to conquer half the world. Lawrence, a scholar-prophet of the modern world, was able again for a time to accomplish this union. It is striking that he, an Occidental,

[1] *Works*, *V*, 48.

[2] T. E. Lawrence, *Revolt in the Desert*, p. v.

should have been able to lead the temperamental Arabs to new victories, and to understand so thoroughly their idealism, and its relation to the world of actuality. In doing so, he was realizing one of Emerson's most "transcendental" beliefs. At the end of his essay on "Experience", Emerson had written: "The true romance which the world exists to realize will be the transformation of genius into practical power." For a time Lawrence transformed pure genius into practical power — and Arabian idealism was his means.

Apparently Emerson did not believe that Mohammed had accomplished this transformation. Perhaps he interpreted practical power in a broader sense — as power over a more highly civilized race. The power of Mohammedanism had been short-lived. The conversation which Emerson records with Mr. Vethake of New York suggests his reason for distrusting the genius of Mohammedanism:

> Mr. Vethake's opinion was that Mahomet had tried power, and Jesus, or, I think, John, persuasion; that Mahomet had felt that persuasion, this John-persuasion, had miserably failed..., and he said, I will try this Oriental weapon, the sword...; and he said to Ayesha, 'I have found out how to work it. This Woman element will not bear the sword; well, I will dispose of woman; she may exist; but henceforth I will

> veil it;' So he veiled Woman. Then the sword could work and eat.... I smelt fagots.... I remembered what I have heard or dreamed, that the most terrific of hierarchs would be a mystic. Beware of Swedenborg *in power*.... Fagots! [1]

Mohammed had gained absolute power for a time — had transformed his religious genius into practical power; but he had done it at the expense of civilization. He had suppressed Woman — the chief civilizing element in society, and had granted full license to the Sword. The result was that his empire did not endure. It lacked the stability of true civilization. It gained inspiration for a time from Mohammed's genius, but soon relapsed into its age-old barbarism, and religion and poetry remained all the civilization of the Arab.

In his essay on "Woman", Emerson again reacted unfavorably, criticizing "Mahomet's opinion that women have not a sufficient moral or intellectual force to control the perturbations of their physical structure." [2] He disliked the religious tyranny of Mohammedanism, with its extreme emphasis on military power and on the warrior. By way of illustrating the opposite sort of power from that of the Arab, he wrote that

[1] *Journals*, VI, 353–4. [2] *Works*, XI, 417.

"The hack is a better roadster than the Arab barb."[1]

Yet for the most part Emerson found the literature and thought of Arabia congenial. It represented only one aspect of life, but it confirmed his own ideas often most unexpectedly. In one of his latest essays, he noted that "even the wild and warlike Arab Mahomet said, 'Men are either learned or learning: the rest are blockheads.'"[2] Perhaps Mohammedanism, even with its snatches of wisdom, and its starts of practical idealism, might be taken as a valuable phenomenon in the history of religious thought. Its genius was real, even if incomplete. As such, Emerson accepted it.

LIST OF ARABIAN BOOKS QUOTED OR READ BY EMERSON

(Number indicates frequency of mention, in years.)

The Koran, or "Mahomet", (7)
(from various sources)
The Arabian Nights, (3)
"Arabian Proverbs", (1)
Abulfeda, *Historia Muslemica*, (1)
Ockley, *History of the Saracens*, (1)
T. Carlyle, *Heroes and Hero-Worship* (essay on Mahomet)

[1] *Works*, VI, 77. [2] XI, 504.

Abd el Kader and General Daumas, *Les Chevaux de Sahara*, (1)

E. Gibbon, *The Decline and Fall of the Roman Empire*; (chapters 50 to 52, especially).

"Arab Ballad".

Akhlak-I-Jalaly, tr. by W. F. Thomson, (London, 1839).

CHAPTER VIII

THE ZOROASTRIAN FORGERIES

THE extent of Emerson's acquaintance with Zoroastrian literature can hardly be determined with accuracy. The problem is one which a summary discussion cannot settle, and this chapter can do no more than outline the evidence. But the problem even thus presented becomes one of exceptional interest.

"Zoroaster" appears in Emerson's Journals, in the annual list of books read, first in 1820, and again in 1822. In 1832 two full pages of the Journals are devoted to Zoroastrianism. Constantly, from 1820 to 1872, over the entire range of his life, Zoroaster reappears in the lists of his reading at frequent intervals. The number of appearances is certainly greater than that of any other single Oriental figure, if we except Plotinus; and so it would appear as though Emerson were more interested in Zoroaster's system of thought, and as though he had come in contact with it earlier than with other Oriental systems. This last statement is partially true, but apparently the rest may be disproved.

Emerson probably did not read any authentic book of Zoroastrianism until 1872, at the very end of his life, when the *Zend-Avesta* is listed. His earliest references are to fragments, to second hand summaries, or to short articles. The great bulk of his references are to two pseudo-Zoroastrian books, both of which have been pronounced utterly false by modern scholarship — although it is only fair to say that Emerson knew that they were possibly unauthentic when he was reading them. These two literary forgeries formed the basis of his knowledge of Zoroaster, and probably are the books to which most of the references in his annual Journal lists are made. They are the sources of all the Zoroastrian quotations in his collected *Works*, and of the bulk of those quotations which he copied into his Journals from time to time. They are (1) the "Chaldean Oracles," or "Oracles of Zoroaster and the Theurgists;" and (2) the "Desatir, or Sacred Writings of the Ancient Persian Prophets."

Before ever reading these works, however, Emerson received his first ideas of Zoroaster from other sources. His first reference in the Journals of 1820–21 is to the "Zendavesta (*apud* Gibbon)." This probably refers to the first volume of Gibbon's *Decline and Fall of the Roman Empire*, in which about five pages are devoted to an explanation of the Zoroastrian system of religion, as it was accepted by King Artaxerxes. Then, six years later, Emerson made use of the Persian pantheon when he wrote: "I am a more cheerful philosopher, and am rather anxious to thank Oromasdes than to fear Ahriman.[1]"

Later, in 1830, when reading in De Gérando's summary of Indian and Chinese systems of philosophy, Emerson apparently makes two direct cross-references to the *Zend-Avesta:* the first being "(*v. L'Oupnek hat*, par Anquetil-Duperron, vol. I, p. 467)" and the second, a page later, "(*La Isechné*, ch. viii, *dans le Zend-Avesta*, par Anquetil-Duperron, vol. I, 2nd part, p. 141)".[2] But upon examination of De Gérando's book, it is evident that Emerson merely copied these cross-references from the footnotes of that work, where they appear verbatim; and that Emerson never read Anquetil's rendering of the *Zend-Avesta*, until, possibly, very much later.

In 1832 we have seen that Emerson filled two complete pages of his Journal with remarks on and quotations from Zoroastrianism, which he

[1] *Journals*, II, 71. [2] *Ibid.*, II, 334–5.

noted, "I am quoting from the *Histoire de l'Académie des Inscriptions*, vol. 37." [1] These quotations seem more authentic than any others on the subject, and probably formed the sound basis on which he added the very precarious superstructure of pseudo-Zoroastrian material, derived from the other two books.

Early in 1844 Emerson copied in his Journals selections from "the 'Chaldean oracles which were either delivered by Theurgists under the reign of Marcus Antoninus, or by Zoroaster.'" [2] And in the last number of *The Dial*, of April, 1844, he inserted, as of the series of "Ethnical Scriptures," further selections from these oracles. His prefatory note from *The Dial* follows:

> We owe to that eminent benefactor of scholars and philosophers, the late Thomas Taylor, who, we hope, will not long want a biographer, the collection of the "Oracles of Zoroaster and the Theurgists," from which we extract all the sentences ascribed to Zoroaster, and a part of the remainder . . .[3]

At a later date Emerson confided to his Journals that "*The Chaldaean Oracles* are plainly all esoteric metaphysics and ethics of a deep

[1] *Journals*, II, 475.

[2] *Ibid.*, VI, 499–500. See also *Ibid.*, 491.

[3] *The Dial*, IV, 529.

thinker speaking after truth, and not after appearance and using whatever images occurred, to convey his grand perception."[1] Finally, near the end of his literary life, he wrote:

> Today I should like to confide to a proper committee to report on what are called the 'Sentences of Zoroaster,' or the 'Chaldaic Oracles'; to examine and report on those extraordinary fragments, — so wise, deep, — some of them poetic, — and such riddles, or so frivolous, others, — and pronounce shortly, but advisedly, what is their true history.[2]

Well, a later scholar has made the following report:

> The wonderful eschatology of the Persian religion made a deep impression on the Hellenic mind at an early date, and this was to bring forth fruit in the development of Gnosticism and Neo-Platonism. Apparently in this way arose the so-called Chaldaean Oracles, which bear the mark of Gnostic and Neo-Platonic mysticism and somewhat recall the Christian forgery of the Sibylline Oracles.
>
> The pseudo-Zoroastrian compositions had but short shrift. The great Porphyry ruthlessly attacked them and suppressed them, and they are lost to us forever... But in the writings of the Neo-Platonic philosophers there lay hid a mass of citations, termed "Chaldaean Logia," or more usually, simply, "Logia," or again, introduced by the formula: "As saith one of the Gods,"

[1] *Journals*, VIII, 534.

[2] *Ibid.*, X, 139.

or even appearing without any introductory phrase whatsoever. These Logia date in general about the end of the second century A.D., and they present to us a heterogeneous mass, now obscure and again bombastic, of commingled Platonic, Pythagorean, Stoic, Gnostic, and Persian tenets..... However trivial the Logia may justly appear to us, they received the serious attention of Iamblichos, Pro-Klos (etc.), while Hierokles, and later Plethon wrote "compends of the Zoroastrian and Platonic systems." [1]

Such were the Zoroastrian oracles, to which Thomas Taylor gave new currency, and which Emerson quoted — being attracted, no doubt, by their close resemblance to the Neoplatonic writings which he liked so much.

And as for the *Desatir:* "The *Desatir*," writes Professor Jackson, "— This curious collection with its commentary, professes to be old; but it is adversely criticized by Wilson." [2] Yet Professor Jackson quoted it in his study, as apocryphal evidence.[3] Another scholar, however, writes as follows:

> Sir William Jones [a prominent orientalist]... who strained at the gnat of the *Zend Avesta*, was destined to swallow the camel of the *Dasatir* — one of the most impudent forgeries ever perpetrated. With the

[1] A. V. W. Jackson, *Zoroaster, the Prophet of Ancient Iran* (New York, 1899), pp. 259–60. (Note by Louis H. Gray.)

[2] *Ibid.*, p. 282.

[3] See pp. 85, 88–90.

original of this egregious work he was, indeed, unacquainted.[1]

And again

he finally accepted the absurd *Desatir* — 'a sacred book in heavenly language' (which proves, in fact, to be no language at all, but mere gibberish, slavishly modelled on the ordinary Persian in which the 'Commentary' is written) — as an ancient historial document of capital importance.[2]

This remarkable book Emerson owned. It came into his hands in the year 1843, probably from the collection of Lane and Wright in the Fruitlands' library. Extracts from it were published as "Ethnical Scriptures" in *The Dial* for July, 1843. It may be that Thoreau actually edited these selections, as they are not attributed to Emerson in G. W. Cooke's bibliography of *The Dial*, but this is rather improbable, and certainly the only current copy of the *Desatir* was Emerson's. The "Preliminary Note" to these "Extracts from the Desatir" read as follows:

"The Desatir or *Regulations*, purports to be a collection of the different Persian prophets, being fifteen in number, of whom Zerdusht, or Zoroaster was the

[1] E. G. Browne, *A Literary History of Persia* (New York, 1902), I, 53.

[2] *Ibid.*, p. 56.

thirteenth... In England attention was first called to the book by Sir William Jones... and the book was afterwards translated from the Persian by Mr. Duncan, Governor of Bombay, and by Mulla Firuz Bin Kaus, a Hindoo, and published at Bombay in 1818."[1]

From the wording of this "Preliminary Note" it seems obvious that Emerson knew of the doubtful authenticity of the *Desatir*, as well as of the Zoroastrian Oracles; and yet he not only used both for purposes of quotation, but also included them in his essay on "Books" in the list of "a class of books which are the best: I mean the Bibles of the world, or the sacred books of each nation... After the Hebrew and Greek Scriptures, which constitute the sacred books of Christendom, these are, the Desatir of the Persians, and the Zoroastrian Oracles; the Vedas and Laws of Menu, [etc.]" Emerson was often uncritical, because he did not care much for accuracy of definition in literary matters, but this listing of two literary forgeries which he himself knew were uncertified, with the established Bibles of the world, seems to reach over the bounds even of Transcendental criticism.

The only explanation possible is that these

[1] *The Dial*, IV, 59.

two were the only Zoroastrian books which he knew, and that he wished to include Zoroastrian Scriptures in the representative list of the Bibles of the world's religions. In at least two other cases he grouped "Zoroaster" with the religious teachers of the world, as — "Socrates, Menu, Confucius and Zertusht" [1] and "Zoroaster, Confucius, and the Indian Scriptures". [2] Also in his Journal comment on the only authoritative statement of Zoroastrianism which he read, he included a long soliloquy on comparative religion, of which the following is a part:

> A strange poem is Zoroastrism. It is a system as separate and harmonious and sublime as Swedenborgianism — congruent. One would be glad to behold the truth which they all shadow forth. For it cannot but be truth that they typify and symbolize, as the play of every faculty reveals a use, a cause, and a law to the intelligent. One sees in this, and in them all, the element of poetry.... the effect produced by making everything outward only a sign of something inward: Plato's *forms or ideas*, which seem almost tantamount to the *Ferouers* of Zoroaster.....
>
> Do we not feel in reading these elemental theories that these grotesque fictions are the gallipots of Socrates, that these primeval allegories are globes and diagrams on which the laws of living nature are explained? Do we not seem nearer to divine truth in these fictions than in less pretending prose?.....

[1] *Works*, VIII, 275. [2] *Ibid.*, VIII, 214.

Prometheus archaic: "Jupiter an upstart."[1]

Here Zoroastrianism takes its place among the ancient religions of the world, and on a par with them. Much subsequent scholarly discussion has been expended in the attempt to discover in how far "These grotesque fictions" actually were "the gallipots of Socrates" and Plato, if indeed they were at all. In Emerson's Essays this comparative spirit is still prominent, when he speaks of "this ineffable cause, which every fine genius has essayed to represent by some emphatic symbol, as, Thales by water,... Zoroaster by fire, Jesus and the moderns by love."

Even the quotations from the *Desatir* and the Oracles which Emerson used in his Essays frequently have something of the same spirit. So in "Character," he quotes from the *Desatir* to illustrate his point:

> The most credible pictures are those of majestic men who prevailed at their entrance, and convinced the senses; as happened to the eastern magian who was sent to test the merits of Zerthusht or Zoroaster. When the Yunani (Greek) sage arrived at Balkh, the Persians tell us, Gushtasp appointed a day on which the Mobeds of every country should assemble, and a golden chair was placed for the Yunani sage. Then the beloved of Yezdam, the prophet Zertusht, ad-

[1] *Journals*, II, 473–5.

vanced into the midst of the assembly. The Yunani sage, on seeing the chief, said, "This form and this gait cannot lie, and nothing but truth can proceed from them."[1]

Here Zoroaster is the type of the great man, and aside from the strange language in which the quotation is couched, the sense is satisfactory. So is it in another quotation from the same book, appearing twice in Emerson's *Works*, which illustrates the familiar theme of "the good old days": "Unspeakably sad and barren does life look to those who a few months ago were dazzled with the splendor of the times. 'There is now no longer any right course of action nor any self-devotion left among the Iranis.'"[2]

In considering the citations which Emerson makes from the Zoroastrian Oracles, the case is not so simple. Some of the sentences are purely Neoplatonic in tone, while some have distinctly the feel of a Persian influence. The first to present itself illustrates both sides, appearing in "The Method of Nature":

> It is remarkable that we have, out of the deeps of antiquity in the oracles ascribed to the half-fabulous Zoroaster, a Statement ... which every lover of the truth will recognize. 'It is not proper,' said Zoroaster, 'to understand the Intelligible with vehemence, but if

[1] *Works*, III, 109. [2] *Ibid.*, III, 59.

you incline your mind, you will apprehend it: not too earnestly, but bringing a pure and inquiring eye.... Things divine are not attainable by mortals who understand sensual things, but only the light-armed arrived at the summit.'

Here everything suggests Neoplatonism except the last metaphor, which has a different tone, suggesting possible Persian influence. And in the essay on "Self-Reliance", the quotation might almost be genuine: "The gods love him because men hated him. 'To the persevering mortal,' said Zoroaster, 'the blessed Immortals are swift.'"

This same tone prevails in most of the other quotations, which may be briefly noted: "'Look not on Nature, for her name is fatal,' said the oracle. The too much contemplation of these limits induces meanness."[1] "'Enlarge not thy destiny,' said the oracle, 'endeavor not to do more than is given thee in charge.' The one prudence in life is concentration; the one evil is dissipation."[2] "According to the old oracle, 'the Furies are the bonds of men;' the poisons are our principal medicines, which kill the disease and save life. In the high prophetic phrase, *He*

[1] Essay on "Fate," VI, 23.

[2] Essay on "Power," VI, 73.

causes the wrath of man to praise him."[1] And in much the same strain is another notation, from the Journals: "Zoroaster has a line saying that 'violent deaths are friendliest to the health of the soul.' Attribute that among his good fortunes to Lincoln."[2]

All the above quotations from the Zoroastrian Oracles have something strong in them. But the following passage is more in the Neoplatonic vocabulary, and is used by Emerson twice, in discussing poetry:

> Our best definition of poetry is one of the oldest sentences, and claims to come down to us from the Chaldaean Zoroaster, who wrote it thus: "Poets are standing transporters, whose employment consists in speaking to the Father and to matter; in producing apparent imitations of unapparent natures, and inscribing things unapparent in the apparent fabrication of the world."[3]

Thus Emerson turned even the forgeries of Oriental literature to account. It is an interesting question whether these works are less valuable through being forgeries. Certainly they are not what Emerson called them — among the Bibles of the world. But, although forgeries,

[1] "Considerations by the Way", VI, 258.

[2] *Journals*, X, 39. It is interesting to see how Emerson developed this idea in his Address on Lincoln. (See *Works*, XI, 335–6)

[3] *Works*, VIII, 19. See also V, 241.

these two pseudo-Zoroastrian books which Emerson used are genuinely Oriental works. They illustrate the Oriental mind in its different phases. The Oracles are often more effective than the genuine Neoplatonic matrix in which they were imbedded. And the *Desatir* is a sort of apocryphal work, quoted by so able a Zoroastrian scholar as Professor A. V. W. Jackson.

So what does it avail to show that Emerson knew no authentic Zoroastrian Scriptures till very late in life, if at all; when the pseudo-Zoroastrian writings helped him to an understanding of the Oriental mind? — Merely this: it shows how little Emerson was "critical" in the modern scholarly sense of the word. He used what he liked in building up his structure of thought, and was thankful for it. It also shows that Emerson's interpretation of Zoroastrianism is not to be trusted, as authentically Zoroastrian. Yet it is to be doubted if Emerson ever attempted to "interpret" any system of thought other than his own. It would be unfair to condemn any man for not being what he never pretended to be.

LIST OF ZOROASTRIAN AND LATER PERSIAN BOOKS READ BY EMERSON

The *Zendavesta*, or *Zend-Avesta*; and "Zoroaster";
a) *apud* Gibbon, *The Decline and Fall of the Roman Empire*;
b)*apud* De Gérando, (a mere mention);
c) *apud Histoire de l'Académie des Inscriptions*;
d) one other version of the *Zend-Avesta*, unidentified, read late in life.

Oracles of Zoroaster and the Theurgists, tr. by Thomas Taylor.

The Desatir, tr. by Mulla Firuz Bin Kaus (Bombay, 1818).

The Dabistan.

CHAPTER IX

CONFUCIUS AND CHINA

My Chinese book does not forget to record of Confucius, that his nightgown was one length and a half of his body.

— EMERSON'S *Journals* for 1843.

CHINESE literature and Buddhism were the only two Oriental systems which Emerson did not wholly welcome. Buddhism epitomized for him the quietism of the East, and its passiveness. Chinese literature epitomized its formalism, and its lack of the progressive element. So, although he gained much from his reading of these two, and although late in life he set aside his aversion to them, his prevailing attitude is decidedly not one of enthusiasm.

His first entry in his Journals concerning China is typical, although it is obviously the expression of an immature mind. It consists of a rhymed couplet:

> I laugh at those who, while they gape and gaze,
> The bald antiquity of China praise.[1]

Emerson had as much opportunity for reading the Chinese classics as the rest of Oriental litera-

[1] *Works*, XI, 637. From his *Journals* for 1824.

ture, and his lack of interest cannot be attributed to his ignorance. He was making the acquaintance of Confucius at about the same time that he was beginning to read Hindu literature. He obtained his first distant impression of both in 1830, when reading the summary of Eastern systems in De Gérando's Cyclopedia; and in his Journals for that year he noted that the Golden Rule was to be ascribed to Confucius, and that the Confucian Classics contained "promising definitions" of Nature, Law, and Instruction.[1] Then in 1834, the "Sheking," or Chinese book of odes, appears among his list of books read during the year.

In 1836, the date of the publication of *Nature*, he first read "Marshman's *Confucius*," and copied many sentences ascribed to Confucius into his Journals.[2] One of these: "How can a man remain concealed" (*bis*), appeared also in his first volume of Essays.[3] In 1837, however, in reading the *Asiatic Journal*, he came in contact with what he labeled "the mountainous nonsense of Chinese diplomacy",[4] and this impression of China is reflected in an essay on "The Conservative" in 1841. In 1838 he was

[1] *Journals*, II, 334.
[2] *Ibid.*, IV, 10.
[3] *Works*, II, 159.
[4] *Journals*, IV, 318.

again reading "Confucius," and quoted in his Journals for that year, "Action, such as Confucius describes the speech of God." Again in 1841 he listed Confucius; and in 1843 he read over the "Sheking." In that year he read for the first time a complete translation of "*The Four Books*" of the Chinese Classics; copying many sentences from them in his Journals. Many of these quotations reappear in his later *Works* — and almost every volume includes one or two illustrative sayings taken from the Chinese Classics. His later Journals, likewise show a continued, although never intense interest in them.

Although Emerson's interest in Chinese literature remained constant, and although he had become interested in it fully as early as he had in other Oriental literature, the differences between the two are striking. He never became wholeheartedly absorbed in the Chinese writings, as he did, for instance, in the Hindu. He never actually incorporated their thought into his own writing, but merely quoted the sayings of Confucius, Mencius, and the rest, externally, as illustrations of his ideas. He always shied away from the merely practical quality of the Confucian precepts, feeling a lack of religious enthusiasm in them.[1] Finally, Emerson felt that the individual figure of Confucius overshadowed the rest of Chinese literature — depriving it for him of some of the popular or human authority possessed by the folk literature of the Hindus and of the other ancient races of Asia.

For Emerson, Confucius was central in Chinese history. Lao-tse he had never read. And yet there is something which recalls the tone of Lao-tse's famous interview with Confucius in Emerson's most typical passage referring to the latter:

> The absolutist is good and blessed, though he dies without the sight of that paradise he journeys after.... But not so..... the middleman who receives and assents to his theories and yet, by habit and talent formed to live in the existing order, builds and prospers among the worldly men, extending his affection and countenance all the time to the absolutists. Ah, thou evil, two-faced half-and-half! how can I forgive thee? Evil, evil hast thou done. Thou it is that confounded all distinctions. If thou didst not receive the truth at all, thou couldst do the cause of virtue no harm. But now the men of selfishness say to the absolutist, Behold this man, he has all thy truth, yet lo! he is with us and ours, — Ah, thou damnable Half-and-Half! choose, I pray you, between God and the

[1] In this context, it is striking that he never seems to have come in contact with Taoism — a philosophy which would doubtless have been more congenial to him than that of Confucius.

Whig Party, and do not longer strew sugar on this bottled spider.

Yes; but Confucius. Confucius, glory of the nations. Confucius, sage of the Absolute East, was a middle man. He is the Washington of Philosophy, the Moderator, the Μηδὲν ἄγαν of modern history.[1]

Here Emerson appears in something of the likeness of Lao-tse, "the old dragon" of Chinese religion, who also denounced Confucius for making terms with the world. But Emerson clearly shows his respect for Confucius even here; and in most other passages, he expresses himself more conservatively, and with greater admiration for the sage. Indeed he copied into his Journals only two years before this, a passage from the Chinese Classics explaining well the action of Confucius:

Chang Tsoo and Kee Neih retired from the state to the fields on account of misrule, and showed their displeasure at Confucius who remained in the world. Confucius sighed and said, I cannot associate with birds and beasts. If I follow not man, whom shall I follow? If the world were in possession of right principles, I should not seek to change it.[2]

Again, in his essay on "Social Aims", Emerson quoted Confucius, without censure, as saying: "If the search for riches were sure to be

[1] *Journals*, VII, 126. [2] *Ibid.*, VI, 403.

successful, though I should become a groom with whip in hand to get them, I will do so. As the search may not be successful, I will follow after that which I love." What Confucius loved was the world of practical ethics and social morality. Emerson felt with distrust his nearness to worldly men, and yet felt the greatness of his search for the right path. One quotation from him he uses twice, and writes: "I will say with Confucius, 'If in the morning I hear of the right way, and in the evening die, I can be happy.'" [1]

But Emerson always felt that this "right way" of Confucius was apt to lead through social convention to formalism. In his Journals he remarked: "The Chinese are as wonderful for their etiquette as the Hebrews for their piety." [2] Shortly before this he had noted with some humor: "My Chinese book does not forget to record of Confucius, that his nightgown was one length and a half of his body." And much later in life he could not resist copying another anecdote of the same tone: "The Englishman in China, seeing a doubtful dish set before him, inquired, 'Quack-quack?' The Chinese replied, 'Bow-wow.'" [3] Whether in humorous or serious

[1] *Works*, XII, 195; and X, 117.

[2] *Journals*, VI, 418.

[3] *Ibid.*, IX, 399.

form, this distrust often recurs — especially in his Journals, where he was more personal, and not writing for publication. In his Essays, the quotations he uses are usually modified, as, for instance, in "Social Aims", where he quotes Confucius twice, noting the second time: "'Eat at your table as you would eat at the table of a king,' said Confucius."

Emerson naturally links Confucius with China in his censure. The man expressed the wisdom of the nation, and when the man was a "middleman", the nation was apt to be even more materialistic and formal. So Emerson coupled him with the "venerable Oriental dynasty" from which he sprang, and with the "mountainous nonsense of Chinese diplomacy... the 'red permit' writ by the vermilion pencil of the emperor,... etc., etc."[1] It is to Emerson's credit that he tried to see the other side of the question: "*Connais les cérémonies. Si tu en pénètres le sens, tu gouverneras un royaume avec le même facilité que tu regards dans ta main.* — Confucius."[2] But even if he should know the sense of the ceremonies, he did not like formalism, and typically in his essay on "The Conservative", he wrote: "I understand well the respect of man-

[1] *Journals*, IV, 318. [2] *Ibid.*, VIII, 516.

kind for war, because that breaks up the Chinese stagnation of society."

In the same vein Emerson censures the Chinese attitude towards woman — an Oriental attitude which he deplored in general. He quotes especially from the "Shiking" to illustrate his point — using an example which Mr. H. A. Giles has requoted in his *History of Chinese Literature*:

> In barbarous society the position of women is always low — in the Eastern nations lower than in the West. "When a daughter is born," says the Shiking, the old Sacred Book of China, "she sleeps on the ground, she is clothed with a wrapper; she plays with a tile; she is incapable of evil or good." [1]

If Emerson saw many things to criticize in Chinese society, and if he never gave his unreserved admiration to Confucius and the literature of the Chinese Classics, he also knew that he could learn much from them. The greater part of the entries in his Journals concerning them are in a tone of respect, and his quotations from them in the Essays are almost all used in confirmation of his own beliefs.

In 1868 he was asked to give a speech at a banquet in honor of the Chinese Embassy then visiting in Boston, and in this short discourse he

[1] *Works*, XI, 414.

naturally brought together his most favorable opinions of China. One of these is especially interesting, since it appears nowhere else in his writings, and since it is the point stressed most by later writers on Chinese civilization — namely, the importance attached to education by the Chinese system.

> China interests us at this moment in a point of politics. I am sure that gentlemen around me bear in mind the bill... requiring that candidates for public offices shall first pass examinations on their literary qualifications for the same. Well, China has preceded us, as well as England and France, in this essential correction of a reckless usage; and the like high esteem of education appears in China in social life, to whose distinctions it is made an indispensable passport.[1]

Besides a respect for education, Emerson attributed to China in this speech the credit for many inventions; for the "respectable remains of astronomic science, and the historic records of forgotten time....... Then," he continued, "she has philosophers who cannot be spared. Confucius has not yet gathered all his fame."

In the following paragraph he listed what he considered the chief contributions of Confucius to the history of thought in the world. First, he

[1] *Works*, XI, 473.

compared the modesty of Socrates to that of Confucius — each of whom "knew that he knew nothing." Second, he wrote: "What we call the *Golden Rule* of Jesus, Confucius had uttered in the same terms five hundred years before." Emerson later referred to this as "the doctrine of Reciprocity." Third, "his rare perception appears in his *Golden Mean*." In this connection we remember Emerson's description of Confucius as "the Moderator, the Μῆδὲν ἄγαν of modern history," and that Emerson's first reference to the Confucian Classics was to the "Invariable Milieu" — or the French translation of the book containing this doctrine. Fourth, Emerson mentioned "his unerring insight, — putting always the blame of our misfortunes on ourselves; as when to the governor who complained of thieves, he said, 'If you, sir, were not covetous, though you should reward them for it, they would not steal.'" Fifth and last, Emerson wrote, "His ideal of greatness predicts Marcus Antoninus." And this sentence he expanded in a further enumeration of Chinese virtues: "their power of continuous labor," and "their stoical economy."

Thus Emerson described the greatness of Confucius. In one way, this description is typical of

Emerson. Under three of the five headings he compared Confucius with other great men — with Socrates, with Jesus, and with Marcus Aurelius. Throughout his writing he did this. Confucius was interesting to him chiefly as the great man — "the sage of the Absolute East." When reading Legge's translation of the Confucian Classics, he noted in his Journal, "I am reading a better Pascal"; [1] and two pages later he wrote, "He anticipated the speech of Socrates, and the *Do as be done by*, of Jesus."

It was the same in Emerson's *Works*. In his essay on "Books," he emphasized the importance of single books to great nations, "as Hafiz was the eminent genius of the Persians, Confucius of the Chinese, Cervantes of the Spaniards." Confucius was one of the wise men of the world. In three separate essays he lists him as follows: — "Socrates, Menu, Confucius, Zerthust;" "Moses, Confucius, Montaigne and Leibnitz;" "Zoroaster, Confucius, and the Indian Scriptures." [2] Thus Confucius appears sometimes in strange company, but always with great men.

Just as Emerson took the personality of Confucius as an example of human greatness, so the largest single topic exemplified by quotations

[1] IX, 533. [2] *Works*, VIII, 214, and 275; XII, 316.

from the Confucian Classics in his writing is that of personal perfection. The first quotation from Confucius to be used in his Works was "How can a man be concealed. How can a man be concealed."[1] In his essay on "Character" he wrote: "I find it more credible... that one man should *know heaven*, as the Chinese say, than that so many men should know the world." And to the same intent he quoted Mencius, the disciple of Confucius, in the essay "Uses of Great Men," writing: "I accept the saying of the Chinese Mencius: 'A sage is the instructor of a hundred ages. When the manners of Loo are heard of, the stupid become intelligent, and the wavering, determined.'" Finally, to illustrate the greatness of Lincoln, in his speech praising the Emancipation Proclamation, Emerson wrote:

> Against all timorous councils, he had the courage to seize the moment; and such was his position, and such the felicity attending the action, that he has replaced government in the good graces of mankind. "Better is virtue in the sovereign than plenty in the season," say the Chinese. 'Tis wonderful what power is, and how ill it is used, and how its ill use makes life mean, and the sunshine dark.[2]

In this last passage, Emerson connects the idea of the great man, with that of power. The

[1] *Works*, II, 159. [2] *Ibid.*, XI, 318.

great man was he who embodied in himself to the highest degree the virtue, the vital force of the universe. His essay "Experience" had expressed this general concept before. But the Confucian Classics do not develop it very markedly. In China, it was the Natural Philosophy of Taoism which best embodied this mystic idea, that the perfect life was the one which was open most fully to the influence of the natural power of the universe. Emerson found the doctrine only at times in the more practical Chinese Classics. In a striking passage of "Experience," however, he borrowed the illustration from them:

> The baffled intellect must still kneel before this cause, which refuses to be named, — ineffable cause, which every fine genius has essayed to represent by some emphatic symbol, as, Thales by water, Aniximenes by air, Anaxagoras by (Νοῦς) thought, Zoroaster by fire, Jesus and the moderns by love; and the metaphor of each has become a national religion. The Chinese Mencius has not been the least successful in his generalization. "I fully understand language," he said, "and nourish well my vast-flowing vigor." — "I beg to ask what you call vast-flowing vigor?" said his companion. "The explanation," replied Mencius, "is difficult. This vigor is supremely great, and in the highest degree unbending. Nourish it correctly, and do it no injury, and it will fill up the vacancy between heaven and earth. This vigor accords with and assists

justice and reason, and leaves no hunger." — In our more correct writing we give to this generalization the name of Being, and thereby confess that we have arrived as far as we can go.

Thus Emerson shared the thought of the Chinese Classics in some cases. He found much in them that he liked. There are many other sentences from them that he thought worth while to copy into his Journals, but that he never used in his *Works*.[1] Yet in general he was interested in China chiefly as one of the ancient civilizations of the world. So he addressed the Chinese Embassy:

> All share the surprise and pleasure when the venerable Oriental dynasty — hitherto a romantic legend to most of us — suddenly steps into the fellowship of nations. This auspicious event, considered in connection with the late innovations in Japan, marks a new era, and is an irresistible result of the science which has given us the power of steam and the electric telegraph. It is the more welcome for the surprise. We had said of China, as the old prophet said of Egypt, "Her strength is to sit still." [2]

Thus, late in life Emerson announced the beginning of the "new era" — when the "Absolute East" and the progressive West were meeting. Emerson was one of the first who took the

[1] See especially *Journals*, IV, 10; VI, 437; and IX, 533.

[2] *Works*, XI, 471.

trouble to acquaint himself with the thought and civilization of this East. He did not always like what he found there. But he ventured as far as he could into its literature; and so, to a degree, he qualified himself to be the announcer and the interpreter of this new era.

LIST OF CHINESE BOOKS READ BY EMERSON

Confucius:

a) *apud* De Gérando; (a mere mention)
b) *apud* "Marshman's Confucius"
c) The *She-King*; (may be same as "b")
d) *The Four Books*, tr. by Rev. D. Collier, (Malacca)
e) "Book of Poetry", *apud* J. Legge.

Sir J. F. Davis, *The Chinese.*
Hue, *Travels in China.*
"Narrative of the Earl of Elgin's Mission to China."

CHAPTER X

EMERSON, ASIA, AND MODERN AMERICA

EMERSON stands on the threshold of modern American literature and thought. In poetry, Whitman early followed him as master, and praised him beyond others. In prose, he has been recognized as one of the greatest American writers. In philosophy, Professor Dewey has asserted that "even if Emerson had no system, none the less he is the prophet and herald of any system which democracy may henceforth construct and hold by". The influence of his personality in his lifetime was probably even greater than the influence of his writings since his death. At all times he has stimulated the minds of men. And he has done this by bringing them something new — new thoughts of his own, and new materials for thought (often Oriental), in his rôle of the American Scholar.

The impetus which Emerson has given toward a new American scholarship has never been fully appreciated. He is probably the founder of the modern school of Comparative Religion, in

America. In his early years he had joined with the other Transcendentalists in promulgating Eastern ideas, and with them he printed the "Ethnical Scriptures" in *The Dial*. Later he wrote to encourage a friend who was publishing a book on the *Religions of the World*. And throughout his own writings the comparative attitude towards the world's religion is prominent. For him Christianity was only one of these, and when he gave up his church in Boston he had already given up the idea of an exclusive Christianity. To the end of his life he sought the wisdom that lay hid "in the treasures of the Bramins and the volumes of Zoroaster". Just before his death he was able to offer some of this wisdom to Harvard students in his course on philosophy. In recent times professors of theology, of Oriental literatures, and of philosophy have alike borne witness to his influence. But the completeness of this may be illustrated by a chance conversation. Once I asked a well-known professor of Comparative Religion in a Western university (a Canadian by birth), what was his attitude toward Emerson, and he answered: "Well, I named my first son after him." — The influence of Emerson has been subtle and far-reaching.

In Comparative Literature as in Comparative Religion, Emerson's ideas have worked powerfully. He made many translations from the Persian poets in his early years, and later he wrote his appreciation of the larger anthology which William Rounsville Alger was publishing of the *Poetry of the East*. After his death, one of the first American handbooks of "Universal Literature", including summaries of the Oriental literatures, was written by Mrs. A. C. L. Botta, a disciple of his. Recently two large anthologies [1] have resulted from this movement, and both of these appropriately include some of Emerson's translations from the Persian poets.

Yet the influence of Emerson on American scholarship has probably been less, and certainly has been less important, than his influence on the creative writing of America. This probably cannot be demonstrated, but the recurrence of ideas or similes in subtly altered forms can furnish hints as to the prevalence of it, and the general trend is clear. First, Emerson's Oriental ideas, such as "Brahma", have stimulated the minds of later American writers directly; and second, more effectively, Emerson's example has

[1] M. Van Doren, *An Anthology of World Poetry* (New York, 1928); and Eunice Tietjens, *Poetry of the Orient* (New York, 1928).

encouraged Americans to seek out for themselves the wisdom of Asia at its sources.

In the case of Whitman both of these influences are apparent. The story of his visit to Concord in 1856 is well known. During this, Thoreau tells us that he asked him if he had ever read the Orientals, and Whitman answered, "No, tell me about them." However, even at this time Thoreau remarked on the Oriental quality of Whitman's poetry, and if Whitman's statement was true, much of his Oriental tinge may be attributed to the influence of Emerson. Later Emerson noted that Whitman's reiterated "I" was much like the "communal 'I'" of Krishna. Certainly Whitman read the Hindu scriptures carefully either just before or just after writing the *Leaves of Grass*, and his Orientalism became more genuine in his later poems. Rabindranath Tagore, on one of his visits to America, declared that "no American has caught the Oriental spirit so well as Whitman". A complete study of Whitman's Orientalism should reveal much; for, like Emerson, he is one of the most "original" of the great American writers.

Emerson, Thoreau [1], Whitman — all shared

[1] A study of Orientalism among the Transcendental group is now in progress at Columbia University, and will soon be published.

the stimulus which the ancient East gave to the progressive thought of America. They started a movement toward Orientalism which has expanded rapidly in American literature, as an increasing number of books testify. Among the moderns many writers have shared in this new Renaissance, and usually, the more original the writer, the more he has derived from it.

In poetry the "translations" from the Chinese by Amy Lowell are well known. These often are rather adaptations, or imitations, built around the suggestion of a Chinese poem, than translations. Chinese poetry itself is so intangible — so incapable of translation into Occidental verse-forms, that it is more an influence than a source. So it may almost be taken as the symbol of the Imagist movement in modern American poetry. It consists of a group of vaguely related word-pictures, made coherent by the imagination of the author and of the reader.

More closely related to the Emersonian tradition are the contemporary Americans who have turned towards Hindu literature. Mr. John Hall Wheelock, for one, has clearly developed his poetry along these lines — in *Dust and Light*, and in his recent writing, especially.

One of his best lyrics is entitled "Nirvana"; and the lines:

> Perpetual death, perpetual rebirth,
> Perpetual passion, and perpetual pain!
> Is there no respite from the wheel of things?

bring in the motive of Buddhism, but end, as in the case of all American poetry, with a larger "Affirmation". And less obviously other American poets, who have come powerfully under the influence of Whitman, have developed Oriental ideas. Mr. Carl Sandburg, for instance, in his poem "Grass", is in the tradition.[1] The ballad, "John Brown's Body Lies A-mouldering in the Grave", with the fundamental idea of Mr. Benét's *John Brown's Body* inherent in it, comes from the same sources of inspiration.

Most original of all contemporary authors, however, and most thoroughly steeped in the tinctures of Hindu literature and thought, is Mr. Eugene O'Neill. He is especially remarkable for his actual visit to Asia, where he absorbed the spirit of the East at first hand. A passage from *Lazarus Laughed* is typical of his writing. Here the theme of the play develops into an expression of the Hindu mysticism of "Brahma": "We will to die! We will to change! Laughing, we

[1] See *American Literature*, I, 233–242 (Nov. 1929).

lived with our gift, now with laughter give we back that gift to become again the Essence of the Giver!... We are the Giver and the Gift." — In *Marco Millions* the theme is American civilization as seen through the eyes of the Orient, and at the end of the play, the four priests of Tao, Confucius, Buddha, and Islam, form a sort of chorus to comment on the action. Here, too, the conduct of Kublai Khan in the presence of Death is curiously reminiscent of that of the Lords of Earth in Emerson's "Hamatreya", and in the *Vishnu Purana.* — In *Strange Interlude* there is something of the Buddhist quietism in the final verdict of: "God bless dear old Charlie, ... who, passed beyond desire, has all the luck at last!" But probably in the imperfectly adapted mysticism of *The Great God Brown*, the fragments of Hindu thought are most apparent. For instance, there is an astonishing incongruity between the Eastern and Western elements in the description of Cybel: "She chews gum like a sacred cow forgetting time with an eternal end." Again Hindu thought appears in the remark of Dion in the same scene: "I'll take the job. One must do something to pass away the time while one is waiting — for one's next incarnation." — And later, when Dion exclaims in a soliloquy: "(with a look of horror) 'Nothing! To feel one's life blown out like the flame of a cheap match...'", and expresses the universal Occidental fear of the concept of Nirvana. Indeed, almost any number of passages like this, recalling Hindu mysticism, may be found in the so-called "realism" of Mr. O'Neill. Perhaps, before the end of the century, a study of "The Orientalism of Eugene O'Neill" may be undertaken.

But what is the significance of this succession of American writers who have come under the spell of Emerson, or of the Oriental literatures which he so valued? What is the significance of his relation to this mysterious and ancient Asia? Does it merely furnish another footnote to the literary history of the world — a history which has already gone into too many volumes? Or does it point towards some larger truth, as yet but dimly seen? As time goes on, I believe that it will become increasingly clear that Emerson, in discovering the Asia of the mind, was guided by that beneficent Fate of which he wrote so much. The first truly American thinker, he first explored this new and untried field of the imagination. He initiated a new scholarship, and a new type of thinking. Like Petrarch, he is the great precursor of a new Renaissance — the

American Renaissance of Orientalism. Just as in the fourteenth and fifteenth centuries the newly discovered riches of Classical literature were stimulating the minds of Italians to a new scholarship and a new creation, so in the nineteenth and twentieth centuries the newly discovered literatures of Asia have been stimulating the leading writers of America to new explorations and new horizons of thought, which shall include the lands of the ancient East.

In this new era in American thought, Emerson has been both scholar and poet. And if it be objected that this Renaissance has not yet truly arrived, and that the literature of Asia is still strange to many American writers, there are two answers. First, the study of the Classics of Greece and Rome did not bring about the Italian Renaissance till more than a century after the time when Petrarch wrote. And more important, Emerson was a prophet whose thought is "saecular" (a word of his own), and whose ideas have tended gradually to realize themselves in the lives of every new generation of men. For the old generations not only pass away into Nirvana, but the new generations also come up out of Nirvana, and nourish themselves on the ideas of the prophets of the past.

APPENDIX

The following list includes all the Oriental titles appearing in Emerson's annual reading lists — which occur in the *Journals*, at the end of the text for each year. The original lists include the "Authors or Books quoted or referred to in Journals", from 1820 through 1874. Often these lists are of exceptional value, having been compiled from the complete, original Journals, many portions of which were not considered worthy of publication in the ten volume edition of 1909:

1820–21

Cudworth (containing many quotations from the Neoplatonists);
Zendavesta (*apud* Gibbon).

1822

Zoroaster (?);
Arabian Nights;
Sir William Jones, *To Narayena.*

1823

"Hindu Mythology and Mathematics", *apud Edinburgh Review.*

1824

None.

1825

None.

1826

None.

1827
None.

1828
None.

1829
None.

1830
Plotinus;
Confucius, Zoroaster, and *Mahabarat*, (*apud* De Gérando).

1831
Plotinus; Porphyry.

1832
Zoroaster, *Zend-Avesta*, *apud Histoire de l'Académie des Inscriptions*;
Cousin (containing remarks on Oriental philosophy).

1833
None.

1834
Plotinus; Hermes Trismegistus;
Vyasa (?)
Sheking (Chinese); Arabian Proverbs.

1835
None.

1836
Code of Menu;
Confucius, *apud* Marshman;
Arabian Nights.

1837
Plotinus;
Calidasa, "Megha Duta", *apud Asiatic Journal*,
Abulfeda, *Historia Muslemica*.

1838

Hermes Trismegistus; Synesius; Proclus; Thomas Taylor;
Institutes of Menu; Sir William Jones, *Translations of Asiatic Poetry*; Buddha.
Zoroaster; Confucius.

1839

Vedas.

1840

Buddha; Vedas; Sir William Jones;
Zoroaster;
Koran; Ockley, *History of the Saracens.*

1841

Plotinus; Hermes Trismegistus; Porphyry, *On Abstinence from Animal Food* (Taylor's translation); Iamblichus, *Life of Pythagoras*; Synesius; Proclus; Olympiadorus;
Vishnu Sarna; Zoroaster; Confucius;
Saadi; Hafiz.

1842

Plotinus; Porphyry; Iamblichus; Synesius, *On Providence*; Proclus; Apuleius.
Vishnu Sarna; Saadi.

1843

Plotinus; Iamblichus; Synesius; Proclus; (Thomas Taylor's translations); Thomas Taylor;
Sheking; *The Four Books* (Chinese Classics);
Vishnu Sarna; Saadi;
Desatir (Persian).

1844

Plotinus; Proclus; Thomas Taylor's translations;
Zoroaster(?), *Chaldaean Oracles.*

1845

Proclus; Ammianus; Stobaeus;
Bhagavat-Geeta; Colebrooke, *On the Vedas*; Vishnu Purana;
Mahomet; Hafiz; *Akhlak-I-Jalaly* (Persian).

1846

Zoroaster; Hafiz; Von Hammer Purgstall, *Translations of Hafiz*;
Chodzko, *Specimens of Ancient Persian Poetry*.

1847

Plotinus; Synesius; Proclus;
Institutes of Menu; Bhagavat-Geeta; Vishnu Purana;
Confucius; Zoroaster;
Saadi; Hafiz; Firdusi; Ferradeddin.

1848

Jamblichus; Heliodorus; Sidonius Apollinaris; Thomas Taylor;
Meghaduta; Vishnu Purana;
Zoroaster; Hafiz; Mahomet.

1849

Desatir, or Sacred Writings of the Ancient Persian Prophets;
Firdusi; Enweri; Saadi; Von Hammer Purgstall, *Geschichte der Schönen Redekunste Persiens*.

1850

Proclus;
Nisami; Enweri.

1851

Vedas;
Firdusi; Saadi; Ammar.

1852

Plotinus; Porphyry; Sidonius Apollinaris;
Saadi.

1853

Thomas Taylor;
Firdousi, *Shah Nameh*.

1854

Plotinus; Dionysius of Alexandria; Porphyry; Iamblichus; Synesius; Proclus; Sidonius;

Bhagavat Geeta; Vyasa;
Saadi, *Gulistan*; Hafiz.

1855
Plotinus; Porphyry; Iamblichus; Proclus;
Rig Veda Sanhita; Vishnu Purana;
Confucius;
Koran; Ali ben Abu Talib; Saadi.

1856
Proclus;
Upanishad; ("Brahma" composed)
Hafiz.

1857
Iamblichus;
Sakoontala, or The Lost Ring, (by Kalidasa);
Hafiz.

1858
Enweri; Hafiz.

1859
Viasa; *Mahabharata*, apud Alger's *Oriental Poetry*.
Plotinus; Apuleius.

1860
Plotinus; Euclid of Alexandria;
Upanishad; Zoroaster;
Hafiz; *Arabian Nights*; Abd-el-Kader;
Narrative of the Earl of Elgin's Mission to China.

1861
Plotinus;
Upanishad; *Mahabharata*; Viasa; Max Müller, *Comparative Mythology*, etc.;
Saadi.

1862

Kalidasa; *Nala and Damayanti*; "Books bequeathed to me by H. D. Thoreau";[1]
Abd el Kader.

1863

Confucius, *Book of Poetry*, apud J. Legge;
D'Herbelot, *Bibliotèque Orientale*;
Saadi; Hafiz; Von Hammer Purgstall.

1864

Bibliotèque Orientale;
Menu; Mahomet.

1865

Vedas; Vishnu Purana;
Zertusht (Zoroaster); Confucius; Mahomet.

1866

Vedas; Hafiz; Mahomet;
Zoroaster(?), *Chaldean Oracles*.

1867

Bhagavat Geeta; Vishnu Purana;
Confucius.

1868

Menu; Bhagavat Geeta; Vishnu Purana;
Hafiz; Confucius.

1869

Proclus;
Zoroaster; the *Dabistan*.

1870

Plotinus; Porphyry;
Menu; Confucius;
Averroës.

---

[1] See list at end of Appendix.

1871
Iamblichus;
Max Müller.

1872
Zend-Avesta; Saadi;
Sir William Jones, *To Narayena*;
Arab Ballad.

1873
Max Müller.

1874
Plotinus.

"BOOKS BEQUEATHED TO ME BY HENRY D. THOREAU."[1]

Rig Veda Sanhita;
First Ashtaka; *Second Ashtaka*; translated by H. H. Wilson.

Sankhya Karika, tr. by H. T. Colebrooke; and the *Bhashya*, or *Commentary of Gaurapada*, tr. by H. H. Wilson.

Lotus de la bonne loi, tr. by M. E. Burnouf.

Le Bhagavata Purana, tr. by M. E. Burnouf.

Institutes of Menu, tr. by Sir Wm. Jones.

Treatise on the Hindu Law of Inheritance, tr. by H. T. Colebrooke.

Select Specimens of the Theatre of the Hindus, tr. by H. H. Wilson.

---

[1] Reprinted from the *Journals* for 1862, IX, 419–20. Some titles abbreviated.

Vol. xv. of the *Bibliotheca Indica*, tr. by E. Roer; *Upanishad.*

Aphorisms of the Nyaya, by Gautama.

Colebrooke's *Miscellaneous Essays.*

Vishnu Purana, tr. by H. H. Wilson.

Nala and Damayanti, tr. by Rev. H. H. Milman.

Aphorisms of the Mimansa, by Jaimini, pamphlet.

Lecture on the Vedanta, pamphlet.

Bhasha Parichchheda, pamphlet.

BIBLIOGRAPHY

This Bibliography includes only the books actually consulted for the purposes of this study and those quoted in it. A bibliographical list of the translations from each Oriental literature which Emerson read will be found at the end of each chapter (beginning with Chapter V); and, in tabular form, in the Appendix.

Part I

Writings of Ralph Waldo Emerson:

1. *The Complete Works of Ralph Waldo Emerson*, 12 vols.; (Boston, 1903; Centenary Edition).
2. *Journals of Ralph Waldo Emerson, 1820–1872*, 10 vols.; (Boston, 1909).
3. *Uncollected Writings, by Ralph Waldo Emerson*, edited by C. C. Bigelow; (New York, 1912).
4. *The Gulistan or Rose Garden of Saadi*, translated by Francis Gladwin; (Boston, 1865). "Preface" by Ralph Waldo Emerson.
5. *Letters from Ralph Waldo Emerson to a Friend* (Samuel G. Ward), edited by C. E. Norton; (Boston, 1899).
6. *Journal of English and Germanic Philology*, vol. XXVI, pp. 475–484; "Unpublished Letters of Emerson", edited by Stanley T. Williams.
7. (Various contributions of Emerson to the *Atlantic Monthly*, and to *The Dial*, have all been reprinted in the above volumes.)

Part II

Translations from Oriental and Neoplatonic Writings, and Related Works read by Emerson. (See also Appendix):

8. *The Bhagavat-Geeta*, trans. by Sir Charles Wilkins; (London, printed for C. Nourse, 1785).
9. Colebrooke, H. T.; *Miscellaneous Essays*, 2 vols., (London, 1837).
10. Cousin, Victor; *Introduction to the History of Philosophy*, trans. by H. G. Linberg, (Boston, 1832).
11. Cudworth, Ralph; *The True Intellectual System of the Universe*, (London).
12. DeGérando, M.; *Histoire Comparée des Systèmes de Philosophie*, 4 vols., (Paris, 1822).
13. Gibbon, Edward; *Decline and Fall of the Roman Empire*, (London, 1821).
14. *Plotinus, Five Books of*; trans. by Thomas Taylor, (London, 1794).
15. *Plotinus, On Suicide*; trans. by Thomas Taylor, (London, 1834).
16. *Plotinus, Select Works of*; trans. by Thomas Taylor, (London, 1817).
17. *The Six Books of Proclus on the Theology of Plato*, trans. by Thomas Taylor, 2 vols., (London, 1816).
18. Taylor, Thomas; various prefaces and introductions to above books.
19. *Upanishads*, trans. by E. Roer, "Biblioteca Indica", vol. XV, (Calcutta, 1853).

Part III

Secondary Sources: —

20. Browne, E. G.; *A Literary History of Persia*, (New York, 1902).
21. Cabot, James E.; *A Memoir of Ralph Waldo Emerson*, (Boston, 1887).
22. Campbell, J. D.; *Samuel Taylor Coleridge*, (London, 1896).
23. Fields, A.; "Mr. Emerson in the Lecture Room", *Atlantic Monthly*, June, 1883, vol. LI.
24. Firkins, O. W.; *Ralph Waldo Emerson*, (Boston, 1915).

25. Giles, H. A.; *History of Chinese Literature* (New York, 1901).
26. Harris, W. T.; "*Emerson's Orientalism*", in Sanborn, *The Genius and Character of Emerson* (q.v.).
27. Harrison, John S.; *The Teachers of Emerson* (New York, 1910).
28. Holmes, O. W.; *Ralph Waldo Emerson* (Boston, 1884).
29. Inge, W. R.; *The Philosophy of Plotinus* (London, 1923).
30. Jackson, A. V. W.; *Zoroaster the Prophet of Ancient Iran* (New York, 1899).
31. Maitra, Herambachandra; "Emerson from an Indian Point of View", in *Harvard Theological Review*, 1911, vol. IV, pp. 403–417.
32. Maulsby, David L.; *Emerson: His Contribution to Literature* (Tufts College, 1911).
33. Mozoomdar, P. C.; "Emerson as Seen from India", in Sanborn, *The Genius and Character of Emerson* (q.v.).
34. *The Platonist: An Exponent of the Philosophic Truth*; ed. by Thomas M. Johnson (St. Louis and Osceola, Mo., 1881 and ff.). A magazine reprinting much of Taylor's Neoplatonic writing.
35. Sanborn, F. B.; *The Genius and Character of Emerson*, Lectures at the Concord School of Philosophy (Boston, 1885).
36. Sears, Clara E.; *Bronson Alcott's Fruitlands* (Boston, 1915).
37. Thoreau, H. D.; *Writings of H. D. Thoreau* (Walden edition, Boston, 1906).
38. Williamson, George; "Emerson the Oriental", in *University of California Chronicle*, 1928, vol. XXX, pp. 271–288.
39. Woodberry, George E.; *Ralph Waldo Emerson* (New York, 1926).

INDEX

INDEX

The following lists do not include titles from the Appendix or Bibliography

Abd-el-Kader, 199, 205, 206
Abu Beker, 208
Abulfeda, *Historia Muslemica*, 198
Academy, 41, 63, 70
Africa, 211
Akhlak-y-Jalaly, 198
Alcott, A. Bronson, 16; visit to England, 48; acquaintance with Messrs. Wright and Lane, English Mystics, 48; deeply versed in Neoplatonism, 73; Emerson's Transcendental friend, 73; thinking influenced by Oriental translations, 100
Alexandria, 15; philosophers of, 39, 50; cosmopolitan city, 40; New Platonists of, 60
Alexandrians, The, "constellation of genius", 55
Alger, William Rounsville, *Poetry of the East*, 22; Emerson's appreciation of his anthology, 22, 249
Ali ben Abu Taleb (Caliph Ali), 166, 181, 205–209, 210
America, 7, 8, 129
American Literature, xiii, 129 *n.*
American scholarship, a new impetus to given by Emerson, 247, 254
Anaxagoras, 244
Aniximenes, 244
Anquetil-Duperron, 11, 219
APPENDIX, 257–263
Arab, the, 165; virtues of, 204; religion all his civilization, 211; dual nature of, unified, 212
Arabia, poetry of, 22; doctrine of fatalism in, 36
Arabian literature, 192, 195–216
Arabian Nights, 197; pure folk tales, 200; encyclopedia of young thinking, 201
Arabian Proverbs, 198; popular, 200; favorites with Emerson, 202
"Aristocracy", 151, 208
Aristotle, 53, 62
Arnold, Matthew, essay on "A Persian Passion Play", 208
Art, Emerson's theory of, 86–90
Aryan race, 18
"Asia", ix, xi, 27, 103
Asia, books of, x; thought of, xi; defined as the Orient, 1; birthplace of humanity, 1, 17; fables of, 6; criticisms of, 7; misery in, 7; old mansion house of, 8; always land of unity and contemplation, 32; a stay-at-home country, 38; of Plato and Emerson, 150;

conquered by Arabs, 211; newly discovered literatures of, 255
"Asia" (poem), 4, and *n.*
Asia and Europe, Emerson's concepts of, differentiated between, 28, 29, 32
Asiatic Journal, 9, 233
Atlantic Monthly, 20, 21, 43 *n.*, 56 *n.*, 62 *n.*
Ayesha, 213

"Bacchus", 163, 169, 188, 189
Bacon, Lord, 55
"Beauty", 24, 93
Behmen, 183
Benét, Mr. S. V., *John Brown's Body*, 129, 252
Berkeley, philosopher, 105
Bhagavat Gîta (Bhagavat Geeta, Bhagvat, Bhagavat Geta, Bhagavad Gita), xii, 18, 23, 33, 77, 98, 106–110, 115, 117, 118, 121, 128, 146, 151, 152
Bible, the book of Christianity, ix; Oriental quality of, x; authors of, not "Asians", xi; passage from in Emerson's Journal, 45
Bibles of the world, 18, 224; various, 51 (*see* Sacred Books, Scriptures)
Bibliography, 265–267
Blake, H. G. O., Emerson's letter to, 109
Blake, William, 179
"Books", 18, 59, 61, 192, 224, 242
Botta, Mrs. A. C. L., *Universal Literature*, 249
Brahma, 113, 114; the supreme, 119; the Over-Soul, 122; unified source of life, 134; and Maia, 135
"Brahma", 19, 97, 104, 109–113, 116, 119–124, 128, 129, 249, 252
Brahmin, 97, 98
Britain, Orientalism in, 28
Browne, E. G., *A Literary History of Persia*, 223
Buddha, 12, 45, 106, 108, 109, 133, 147, 149, 150, 253
Buddhism, 31, 46, 107, 144, 146–148, 232
Buddhist hospitality, 106, 147; quietude, 253
Burns, 191
Byron, 194

Cabot, J. E., *A Memoir of Ralph Waldo Emerson*, 5 *n.*
Calidasa, 12 (*see* Kalidasa)
Campbell, J. D., *Samuel Taylor Coleridge*, 53 *n.*
Carlyle, essay on Mohammed in *Heroes and Hero Worship*, 198
Cervantes, perpetually modern, 192; eminent genius of the Spaniards, 242
Chaldea, 10, 22, 40
"Chaldean Oracles", 15, 218, 220, 221
Chaucer, 170
Child, Lydia Maria, *The Progress of Religious Ideas*, 22
China, 9, 12, 22, 46, 232, 240, 245
Chinese Classics, 18, 234, 236, 239, 245

Chinese Embassy, speech at, in Boston, 239, 245
Chinese system, 10; literature, 200, 232, 234; diplomacy, 233, 238; etiquette, 237; virtues, 241; poetry, 251
Chodzko's *Specimens of Ancient Persian Poetry*, 161
Christianity, Bible the book of, ix; religion of the Occident, ix
Christians, 203
Civilization, ancient Eastern, 3, 17; of Europe, 3
Classical literature, 255
Cloud-Messenger, *Megadhuta*, 110
Colebrooke, H. T., *Miscellaneous Essays*, 104 *n.*, 107, 109
Coleridge, 53, 71, 95, 96, 100
"Compensation", 99, 146
Compensation, law of, 181
Conduct of Life, The, 23, 24, 64, 208
Confucius, teachings of, 11; writings read in 1837 by Emerson, 12; wisdom of, 18; religious teacher, 225; quoted by Emerson, 234, 237; the Washington of Philosophy, 236; greatness of, 240; the Moderator, 241; a better Pascal, 242; personal perfection of, 243; priest of, in O'Neill play, 253
Confucian Classics, 233, 241, 244; Legge's translation of, 242
Cooke, G. W., bibliography of *The Dial*, 223
Cousin, Victor, *Introduction to the History of Philosophy*, 29 *n.*, 96
Cudworth, Ralph, *Intellectual System of the Universe*, 44, 55, 68, 139, 140

Dæmonology, 78
Daumas, General, and Abd-el-Kader, 205
"Days", 163, 186–188
Death, 125, 253
Deity, 29, 80, 153 (*see* God, Gods)
De Gérando, *Histoire Comparée des Systèmes de Philosophie*, 42, 44, 106, 219, 233
Dervishes, 187, 188 and *n.*
Desatir (Dasatir) or *Regulations*, 18, 218, 222; "Extracts from the Desatir", Preliminary Note to, 223, 224; authenticity doubtful, 224; apocryphal work, 230
Dewey, Professor, 247
Dial, The, 21, 22, 108, 161, 162, 220, 223, 248
Divinity School Address, 12, 153
Duncan, Governor of Bombay, trans., 224

East, absolute, x; "melodramatic mystery" of, xi; "mysterious", 3, 4; life in, simple, 33, 34; religious writings of, 115; meets West, 245.
Eastern and Western thought, 100
Edinburgh Review, 6 and *n.*, 106, 154
Egypt, 12, 22, 40
El Dorado, 5, 7, 10
Ellis, Havelock, *The Dance of Life*, 101 *n.*

"Eloquence", 201
Emanations, 42
Emancipation Proclamation, Emerson's speech in praise of, 243
Emerson, Ralph Waldo, his interest in Asia, ix–xii; not an Orientalist from the outset, 2; formative years in comparative ignorance of Oriental thought, 10; an Orientalist in earnest in 1845, 13; rôle of American Scholar, 18, 132, 247; interpreter of Oriental thought, 19; love for the Orient, 35; expression of Orientalism in his writings, 43; Neoplatonism his introduction to Orientalism 44; much interested in it by 1831, 45; his enlarged knowledge of the Orient, 46; relative importance of Neoplatonism and Orientalism in his thought, 49; admiration of and praise for Thomas Taylor, 54–56; high appreciation of Proclus, 58, 59; revulsion from Neoplatonism, 59; definition of "Platonists", 60; read them not for opium but inspiration, 62; his Neoplatonic borrowings, 67, 71; larger theory of Nature, 69; his "Orphic poet", 72–74; doctrine of the Over-Soul, 75; metaphor of the spiritual light, 76; mid-world affirmed best, 81; his theory of Art from Plotinus, 89; Thoreau's bequest to, 110; Yankee and Oriental, 124; the Literary Artist, 132; progress of his mind, 141; repelled by concept of Nirvana, 149, 150; admiration for Hindu thought qualified with Yankee shrewdness, 155; not "a geographical mistake", 156; Hafiz and Saadi his ideal poets, 178, 179, 182; appreciation of feminine force of the world, 180; gave absolutely unqualified praise to no writer, 182; criticism equally applicable to Shakspeare and the Persian poets, 184; conversation with Mr. Vethake, 198, 213; belief often corresponded with Mohammed's, 206; literature and thought of Arabia congenial, 215; held system of education in China in high esteem, 240; influence on later American literature and thought, 247–249; on American creative writing, 249–254; discoverer of the Asia of the mind, 254; scholar and poet in new era in American thought, 255
"Emerson from an Indian Point of View", with extracts, 157, 158
Emerson, Edward, 10, **25**, 58, 186; *Notes*, 90, 94 *n.*
Emerson, Ellen Tucker, 45
Emerson, Lidian, "Mine Asia", 30
Emerson, Mary Moody, "Tnamurya", 4; correspondence of aunt and nephew, 4, 5, 7, 62, 103; influence on Emerson of

her acquaintance with books of the East, 4, 6
Emerson, Waldo, 30
Emersonian, 74, 94, 152, 173
England, 9, 53, 56
English Traits, 28, 54
Essays, First Series, 11, 12, 56, 105, 139, 140, 233
Essays, Second Series, 13, 105, 147, 180
"Ethnical Scriptures", series of, 22, 223, 248
Europe, xi, 7, 8, 28, 32
Everett, Edward, 3, 73
Evil the absence of good, 82–86, 235
"Experience", 81, 83, 84, 213, 244

Fatalism, Mohammedan feeling for, 24; is Orientalism, 37
"Fate", 23, 24, 37, 104, 141–144, 146, 165–167, 228 *n.*
Fate, Oriental acceptance of, 36, 37; Hindu theory, 142–146; symbol of Life, 169
Ficinus, Marcilius, 55
Firdousi, *Shah Nameh*, 162, 180; Persian Homer, 190
Firkins, O. W., quotation from, 51; *Ralph Waldo Emerson*, 51 *n.*
"Fragments on the Poet" and "The Poetic Gift", 162, 176, 177, 178 *n.*, 193
Freedom, idea of, 24, 37
"Friendship", 99
Fruitlands, library at, 223

Gay, Martin, 4
Genius and Character of Emerson, The, 156 *n.*, 157 *n.*
German Idealism, 94
Gibbon's *Decline and Fall of the Roman Empire*, 192, 197, 219
"Gifts", 187 *n.*
Giles, H. A., *History of Chinese Literature*, 239
Gladwin, Francis, trans., *The Gulistan or Rose Garden of Saadi*, 21 *n.*
Gnosticism, 221
God, 71, 87, 89, 139, 172, 187, 188, 209, 210, 235
Gods, 330 million, 7; of the mind, 31; on their thrones, 64; life of, 65; myths concerning, 72; demi-gods and men, 79; the strong, 118
Goethe, 16, 95, 100, 110, 190
"Goethe", 152
Greece, 6, 40
Greek fables, 6; tongue, 39; mythology, 138
Greeks, late, 39; later, 40; greatest thinkers, 57; philosophy of, 131
Gulistan, The, or Rose Garden of Saadi, 21 and *n.*, 23, 161, 162, 165, 192; Emerson's Preface to first American Edition, 21, 23, 37 *n.*, 162, 165, 185, 192, 193

Hafiz, 36, 48, 49, 51, 93, 162–169, 171–175, 177–185, 187, 189–194, 242
"Hamatreya", 19, 104, 109, 122, 124–127, 129, 151, 253; Yankee element in, 124, 125, 127; Earth Song in, 125, 126

Harris, W. T., *The Genius and Character of Emerson*, 118, 77 *n.*, 121 *n.*
Harrison, John S., exponent of Emerson's Neoplatonism, 51, 52; *The Teachers of Emerson*, 40, 66, 97, 98, 40 *n.*, 68 *n.*, 71 *n.*, 72 *n.*, 77 *n.*, 79 *n.*, 89 *n.*, 98 *n.*, 102 *n.*, 121 *n.*, 130 *n.*, 140 *n.*, 188 *n.*
Harvard Theological Review, 111 *n.*, 157 *n.*, 158 *n.*
Harvard University Library, Thomas Taylor's translations acquired by, 48
Hatem Tai, 203
Haukal, Ibn, *Oriental Geography*, 198, 203
Heetopades, 106
Hegel, 95–97
Heraclitus, 57, 131
Herbert, 51
Hermes Trismegistus, 57
"Heroism", 203, 204
Hilali, *The Flute*, 181
Hindu (Hindoo), 121; mythologies, 5, 103; religion, 6, 154; works, 20; philosophy, 41, 47, 103, 110; poem, 147; literature, 98, 104, 105, 110–112, 161, 233, 234; verse, 103; theology, 122; books, gymnastics for the mind, 133; widow, 137; superstition, 138; soul, 139; fables, 141; definition of law, 145; attitude towards law, 152; students, attitude of towards Emerson, 155
Hinduism, 121, 148
Hindus (Hindoos), 18, 103, 161
Hindustan, 22, 103, 112
Histoire de l'Académie des Inscriptions, 220
"History", 12, 105, 140
Hoar, Elizabeth, 90, 107, 189
Holmes, Oliver Wendell, quotations from, 50; *Ralph Waldo Emerson*, 51 *n.*
Homer, 170, 192

Iamblichus (*see* Jamblichus), 46, 47, 50, 90, 91, 102, 222; *Dæmonology*, 78
Illusions (*see* Maia), 24, 34
"Illusions", 23, 24, 64, 98, 104, 122, 123, 129–132, 167
"Immortality", 25, 104, 119, 136, 210
India, ritual of, 3; land of devout and contemplative East, 12; stories from, 18; philosophy of, 22; under charm of Fatalism, 36; travellers from, 40; sages of ancient, 157
Indian fables, 24; literature, 104, 106, 143; influence, 105; legend, 139
Indra, god of the storm, 118
Inge, Dean W. R., *The Philosophy of Plotinus*, 79, 84, 85
"Initial, Dæmonic and Celestial Love", 79
Intellect, 31, 80
Islam, 208; foundation of, 209; warriors of, 210; knowledge of, 210; priest of, in O'Neill play, 253

Jackson, A. V. W., *Zoroaster, the Prophet of Ancient Iran*, 22 *n.*; Zoroastrian scholar, 230

Jamblichus (*see* Iamblichus), 39, 43, 59
Japan, 18; innovations in, 245
Jesus, and Plotinus, 62; Golden Rule of, 241; and Confucius, 242; symbol of, 244
Jews, literature of, ix
"John Brown's Body Lies A-mouldering in the Grave", 252
Jones, Sir William, trans. of "Narayena", 5; "Translations of Asiatic Poetry", 45; prominent Orientalist, 222, 224
Judea, historic, ix
Julian, Emperor, praise of Iamblichus, 59

Kalidasa (*see* Calidasa), 17
Kant, Immanuel, of Königsberg, 95, 96
Katha Upanishad (*see* Upanishad), 98, 110, 111, 116–118
Kaus, Mulla Firuz Bin, trans., 224
Koran, the, 12, 165, 166, 172, 173, 183, 184, 195, 196, 198, 199, 205–207, 209, 210
Krishna, 123, 250
Kurroglou, Arabian story of, 203, 204

Lane, English Mystic, 16, 223
Lanman, Professor, of Harvard, 111, 116
Lao-tse, 235
Lawrence, T. E., 212; *Revolt in the Desert*, 212 *n.*; transformed pure genius into practical power, 213
Letters and Social Aims, 162
Letters of Emerson to a Friend, 107 *n.*, 154 *n.*, 155
Lincoln, 229; address on, 229 *n.*; greatness of, 243
Lists of books quoted or read by Emerson: Hindu, 159; Persian, 194; Arabian, 215; Zoroastrian and later Persian, 231; Chinese, 246 (*see* Appendix)
Locrus, Timæus, 140
Longfellow, "The Leap of Roushan Beg", 203
Love and Friendship, common appreciation of by Emerson and Persian writers, 181
Lowell, Amy, "translations" from the Chinese, 251
Lowes, Professor J. L., *The Road to Xanadu*, 112
Lucanus, Ocellus, 90

Mahabharata, 104, 106
Mahomet (*see* Mohammed), 207, 210
Maia (*see* Maya), Hindu goddess, 122, 123, 132
Maitra, Herambachandra, 155, 157, 158
Malloy, Charles, 151
"Man the Reformer", 211
"Manners", 99
Marco Millions, American civilization through eyes of the Orient, 253
Marcus Antoninus, 220, 241, 242
Marshman, *Confucius*, 233
Maulsby, D. L., *Emerson*, 112, 107 *n.*, 153 *n.*

Maya (*see* Maia), Hindu conception of, 98, 134
Mead, Professor G. R. S., 42
Mencius, wisdom of, 18; quoted, 234; disciple of Confucius, 243; generalization of, 244
Menu, Laws of, 11, 12, 18, 33, 45. 106, 108, 129 *n.*, 224, 225
Metempsychosis (*see* Transmigration), 135, 136, 138
Milton, 54
"Mine Asia", ix, 30
Mirandola, Picus, 55
Mohammed, 165, 166, 196, 198, 200, 204, 209, 212–215
Mohammedanism, fatalism of, 166; Hafiz and Saadi partially freed from, 171; philosophic side of later, 198; philosophy of, 199; religious utterances of 200; absolute single-mindedness typical of, 208; absolute seriousness and sincerity demanded by, 209; direct appeal of inspiring, 211; religious tyranny of, 214; its genius real though incomplete, 215
Montaigne, 17, 51, 192
Mozoomdar, Protap Chunder, quoted, 25; address, 155, 25 *n.*, 156 *n.*

"Narayena", translation by Sir William Jones, 5
Nature (Emerson's first published work), 11, 12, 23, 63, 67, 69–71, 74, 75, 77, 80, 85, 86, 90, 94, 104, 106, 108, 153
Nature, two poles of, 31; source of great men, 55; foundations of, 57, 70; venerable and organic as, 62; an image of wisdom, 63; laws of, Neoplatonic, 70; not fixed, 74; and Spirit, parallelism between, 77, 78; bruteness of, Neoplatonic theory, 83, 84; Emerson's description of, 85; Plotinus' theory of, 87; is language to inspired poet or artist, 90; the external world, 133; Fate a force of, 144; will not be a Buddhist, 147; typical Hindu child of, 150; Emerson's theory of, 153; is language for ideal poet, 176; value even of low, 177; Hafiz and Saadi had seen, 178; beauty in, 179
"Nature as Discipline", 130
"Nature as Language", 69, 71, 75, 90, 148
Neoplatonic literature, xi; ideas, 40; philosophy, 43; mysticism, prophecies of, 72; doctrine, 74; fable of dæmonic realm, 78; thought, overtone of, 90; books, 99; matrix, 230
Neoplatonism, xi, 2, 4, 15, 16, 40, 41, 43, 44, note p. 47, 48, 51, 52, 63, 65, 66, 74, 81, 86, 91, 93, 94, 98–100, 102 *n.*, 121, 221, 227
Neoplatonists, x, xi, 15, 39, 40, 41, 47, 48, 53, 57, 59, 60, 67, 74, 98, 129, 161
Nirvana, 25, 252, 255

Occident, ix, xi, 26, 28, 37, 210
Ockley's *History of the Saracens*, 198
"Ode to Beauty", 93

Olimpiodorus, 57
Omar, 205, 208, 209
Omar Khayyam, 190
O'Neill, Eugene, *Lazarus Laughed*, 252; *Marco Millions*, *Strange Interlude*, *The Great God Brown*, 253; Hindu mysticism in, 254
"Oracles of Zoroaster and the Theurgists", 218, 220, 230 (*see* Zoroastrian Oracles)
Orient, vii, viii; mysterious and unknown, 1, 17; "Mother India" phase of, 6; Emerson saw attractive side of, 7; aversion to predominant later, 9; religion and philosophy in, 11; vague references to, 12; not romantically marvelous, 28; its poetry, philosophy, and thought, 35
Oriental Literature, x-xii, 2; Emerson's wide interest in, 23; attractive to Occidentals, 35; theory and practice of, 37; philosophy of, 43; doctrines of Neoplatonism in, 97; forgeries of, 229, 232
Oriental, mystery, xi, 9; ideas, xi, 14, 23, 24; life and literature, 2, 34; systems, 10, 44; books, antiquity of, 18; countries, wisdom of, 22; characteristics, 36; largeness, 107; temperament, 187; Superlative, 203
Orientalism, 12, 13, 14, 16, 21, 30, 37, 43, 110, 121, 255
Orientals, 1, 26, 32, 37, 38
Orphic, doctrine of the, 73, 74
Othman the Turk, 205, 208
Over-Soul, the, 75–78, 88, 89, 120, 122, 129, 134
"Over-Soul", 50, 76, 77, 80, 86, 99, 120, 121; source of title, 42, 77, 121

Paradise, 171, 196, 204, 207, 210
Parmenides, 98
Perry, Bliss, Dedication, xiii
Persia, 12, 22, 36, 40, 103
"Persian Poetry", 21, 33, 37, 103, 161 *n.*, 162, 164, 168, 174, 181, 183, 192
Persian poetry, 93, 94, 161–194, 195, 231
Persian poets, 12, 17, 20, 47, 131, 161, 164–168, 171, 176, 181, 188, 196, 249
Petrarch, 254, 255
Plato, x, xi, 3, 4, 8, 14–16, 32, 36, 39, 40, 41, 50–54, 57, 60–62, 65, 70, 98, 129, 131, 148, 200, 225
"Plato", 20, 28, 29, 43, 55, 104, 109, 115, 119, 120, 123, 198, 209
Platonism, 15, 40, 98
Platonist, The, 53 *n.*
Platonists, 3, 40, 43, 55
Plethon, 222
Plotinus, 4, 39–45, 47, 48, 50, 51, 57, 58, 62, 63, 65, 68, 70, 71, 75–77, 79, 85, 90, 92, 101, 131, 153, 217
Plotinus, "Art", 87; parable of the stone blocks, 88; *Select Works*, *On Suicide*, 89 *n.*; *Dance*, 101
Poems, 181, 183
"Poet, The", 88, 90–93, 94, 99, 153

"Poetry", 71
"Poetry and Imagination", 133, 148
Porphyry, 39, 43, 45–47, 50, 51, 76, 101, 221
"Power", 24, 166, 167, 228 *n.*
Principles, feminine, 8, 38, 46; masculine, 31; divine, 79
"Problem, The", 89
Proclus, 31, 39, 41, 43, 45–47, 50, 51, 57, 58, 61, 72, 83, 90, 91–93, 101, 102, 222
Proper names, Oriental, spelling of, x; mystery of, xiii
Purgstall, Von Hammer, *Anthology of Persian Poetry*, 161, 166; Emerson's translations from, 162, 196 (*see* Von Hammer)
"Pythagorean Fragments", 90
Pythagoreans, 140
Pythologian Society, 4

Reading-lists, annual, 10, 47 *n.*, 105–107, 190 (*see* Appendix)
"Reminiscence", Plato's doctrine of, compared to Hindu idea of transmigration of souls, 44, 138
Renaissance, new, 251, 255; Italian, 255
Representative Men, 14, 16, 109, 183
Riley, Woodbridge, *History of American Thought*, 70
Roer, E., trans., *Biblioteca Indica*, 116
Romance, Mother of Knowledge, 7
Rome, 40, 89, 211
Rudra, 134
Saadi, 21, 33, 36, 47, 162–165, 169–173, 175, 176, 182–184, 190–194; Saadi's *Gulistan* (*see* Gulistan)
"Saadi", 20, 161, 162, 174, 175, 177, 192
Saccas, Ammonius, 40, 41
Sacred books, 18; of the Orient, 22; India, 106
Sanborn, F. B., ed. 112, 118 *n.*, 121 *n.*
Sandburg, Carl, "Grass", 129, 252
Sanskrit, 12, 111
Saracen empire, 197; religion, 211
Schelling, 51, 95, 96, 142
Scriptures, Eastern, 16; Hebrew and Greek, 18; Indian, 115, 225; Hindu, 145, 154; Greek, 224; Hebrew, 224; Zoroastrian, 225
Sears, Clara Endicott, "Bronson Alcott's Fruitlands", 49 *n.*
"Self-Reliance", 99, 206, 228
Self-Reliance, doctrine of, 151, 152, 173, 174
Shakspeare, 17, 62, 192; Hafiz, Saadi and, 182; and Hafiz, 169, 183, 191
"Shakspeare, or the Poet", 169, 183, 207
"Sheking", Chinese, 11, 233, 234, 239
Sibylline Oracles, Christian forgery of, 221
Sin, definition of, 83
Society and Solitude, 132
Socrates, 76, 225, 241, 242
"Song of Nature", 62
"Sphinx", 104, 127, 128

Spirit, 70, 74, 79, 80
Stoics, 222
Sufi mysticism, 164 *n.*
"Superlative, The", 25, 34, 36
Swedenborg, 16, 31, 183, 207, 214, 225
"Swedenborg", 138, 139, 141, 152, 170
Synesius, 45, 46, 50, 57, 59

Tagore, Rabindranath, 250
Taoism, 235; natural philosophy of, in China, 244, 253
Taylor, Jeremy, 55
Taylor, Thomas, 15, 40, 52, 54, 55, 220, 222; translations of, 43, 45, 46, 48, 53, 54, 71 *n*, 76, 90, 101
Thoreau, 22, 25, 49, 100, 128 *n.*, 129, 223, 250, 262, 263
"Thought", 80
Tietjens, Eunice, *Poetry of the Orient*, 249 *n.*
Transcendental criticism, 224; group, Alcott and Emerson, most intellectual of, 95; study of Orientalism among, 250; movement, Emerson's friendship with chief members, 48; origin of term ascribed to Kant, 96; school of thought and Neoplatonship, relationship between, 94
Transcendentalism, usually considered a literary movement, 94; Neoplatonists precursors of, 95; relative importance of the German and Neoplatonists to, 96; German school parallel to and separate, 97; more than a philosophic idealism, 100
Transcendentalists, 49, 95, 96, 248
Transmigration (*see* Metempsychosis), 135–142, 144

"Uncollected Writings", 162, 182 *n.*
Unity, 115, 134
Upanishads, the, 18 (*see Katha Upanishad*)

Van Doren, M., *An Anthology of World Poetry*, 249 *n.*
Von Hammer, 190, 199, 203, 208 (*see* Purgstall)
Vedanta, 144, 145
Vedas, 12, 18, 104, 106–109, 115, 134, 224
Veeshnu (Vishnu) *Sarma*, 12, 106, 108; Emerson's Introduction to, 108
Vishnu, 127, 132, 133, 141, 142, 153
Vishnu Purana, 18, 107, 108, 110, 114–117, 124, 126, 253
Vyasa (Viasa), 11, 12, 104, 106, 107

"Ward's Chinese Book," 31, 46
West, xi, 28, 38, 99, 209
Wheelock, John Hall, 251, 252
Whitman, 129; follower of Emerson, 247; Tagore's tribute to, 250; his influence on modern American poets, 252
Wilkins, Sir Charles, trans., 115 *n.*
Woman, conversation on, 31; passages on, 46; inspirational

quality of, 180; veiled, suppressed, 214; Emerson censures Chinese attitude toward, 239
Woodberry, G. E., *Ralph Waldo Emerson*, 51 *n.*
"Woodnotes", 93
Wordsworth, 95, 100, 157
"World Soul", 77
"Worship", 24, 145, 171, 209
Wright, English Mystic, 16, 233
"Wrong, spectral", 84

Xenophanes, 131

Yama, God of death, 118
Yankee, 37, 124, 125, 127, 135
Yoganidra, 130

Zend Avesta, 47, 218, 219, 222
Zertusht (*see* Zoroaster), 223, 225, 226
Zoroaster, 11, 12, 15, 45, 220, 225–229, 244; volumes of, 5, 248; literature of, 217; *Ferrouers* of, 225
Zoroastrian Oracles, 18, 224, 227
Zoroastrianism, 11, 219, 225, 230